Experimenting with Seeds and Plants

About the Book

Plants seem to take care of themselves very well—too well, in fact, when it comes to weeds in a garden. If we know what to do, however, we can often persuade plants to go our way instead of their own.

This book offers a wide choice of experiments that help reveal plant secrets. The reader is encouraged to develop his own "plant laboratory" for the purpose of finding out about plant life. Step-by-step procedures and descriptions are clearly written as guidelines for the young scientist as he conducts inquiries into the how and why of this engaging study.

Experimenting
With Seeds
And Plants

by Ware Budlong &

Mark H. Fleitzer

G. P. Putnam's Sons New York

FOUNDED 1838

GPPS

c. 1

Contents

SECTION I

Plants seem to take care of themselves very well—too well, in fact, when it comes to weeds in the garden and lawn mowing. If we know what to do, however, we can often persuade plants to go our way. We can make a plant turn a corner. We can take two plants of the same kind in our own garden, indoors or outdoors, and make one a dwarf and the other a giant.

There are wide choices among the interesting things to do with plants. We can have our own plant laboratories to carry out experiments that will help us find out about plant secrets. We can start a school of plants, teaching them new things. And we can make special small homes for them, with their own private climates, so seeds will sprout ahead of time and seedlings will flourish.

Your Own Plant Laboratory

Starting a plant laboratory is easy. The first step is choosing a location for it. The best place might be a corner of your room or a section of the basement. Your decision will depend on the amount of space available, on the nearness of an electric outlet for good lighting, and on getting an OK from the family. You will need no more furnishings than a worktable, a chair or stool, and shelves to hold equipment.

Equipment is collected with ingenuity, not money. As you select experiments to do, you will notice what is needed. Usually the necessary items will be things that you can find around the house and can adapt for your purposes. You may want a shoe box, a peanut butter jar, large paper clips, or the plastic that covered a garment from the cleaner. Some of the most effective experiments make use of familiar objects such as coffee cans and mailing tubes.

Obviously it is important to explain to the family what you are planning and to get their interest and cooperation. You probably know this, but here are two reasons for remembering it. If you tell why you need something and get it officially, you will avoid the indignation that might result from using the last sheet of aluminum foil in your mother's kitchen drawer or the last bit of scotch tape from your father's desk. Also, as your experiments show dramatic results, your family will be an enthusiastic audience.

There are several easy ways to start a well-equipped laboratory. One is to make out a list, to be posted somewhere in the house, of the jars and boxes and other things you will need. These can be turned over to you as they become empty.

Another way of equipping the laboratory is to choose several experiments from those in this book and to start collecting the equipment needed for them while the first experiment is progressing. This will save you, when you start a later experiment and need a coffee can, from being told, "I threw it out yesterday." Instead, your shelves will be well supplied, ready for the future.

A third way to gain equipment is to have a stockpile of duplicates—jelly glasses, large rubber bands, plastic sheets cut from those garment covers, neat strong cartons of several sizes, and shallow cans such as the ones tuna fish comes in. Then you will have something to trade with another person who is also setting up a laboratory. You may find that, as you show your more dramatic experiments, some of your friends will decide to have their own laboratories, too.

Some of the experiments and activities in this book are classic projects, done by many people over many years; some are new; some have been developed by students aged eleven and twelve. Following are several good experiments to start your laboratory work.

1. EXPERIMENT

This will show what happens when seeds get a proper supply of water. You will compare the results of trying to sprout seeds with and without water.

Needed: Two plastic pill bottles with caps of the push-on type, and a seed package of beans from the supermarket.

Directions: Fill one bottle with beans alone, the other with beans and water. To prevent unwanted growths, first soak the seeds in a fungicide solution. Make the solution about twice the volume of the seeds. After about twenty minutes, throw away the fungicide solution, wash the seeds with water, and dry them. This will make the experiment more attractive to the nose and eyes. Fasten the caps firmly on the bottles. Set the two bottles on your table and check them regularly to see how the beans will sprout.

In a few days one of the bottles will split or its cap will fly off. Why? Compare the beans in both bottles to see the result of adding water.

Pill bottles showing results of pressure of growing seeds. Bottle second from left contains seeds only; no water was added.

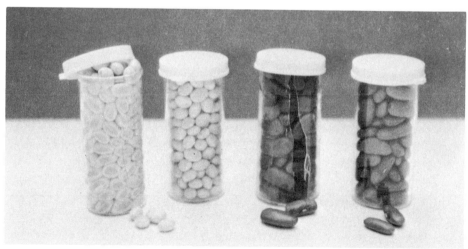

2. EXPERIMENT

This experiment will show seed germination. You will be able to see the seed in its stages of growth.

Needed: One-third of a regular milk carton. Some bean seeds from the supermarket. Be sure to get the seeds that are sealed in a package. Soil is needed, also some Saran Wrap.

Directions: Use the bottom one-third of a milk carton. Slice down two corners so that one side falls down but remains hinged at the bottom. Allow this side to remain in the down position. Cover this open side with Saran Wrap. Use scotch tape or masking tape to secure the Saran Wrap. Swing back the lowered side of the milk carton. Place an elastic band around the carton to hold this side in place. Fill three-fourths of the carton with soil and in it, next to the Saran Wrap, place some bean seeds. Cover these seeds with about one bean seed thickness of additional soil. Punch a few drainage holes in the bottom of the carton. Water only enough to keep the soil moist.

To see the seeds germinate, merely remove the elastic band. Let down the side of the carton, and peek in at your growing seeds.

This peekaboo seed germinator was invented by a sixth-grade girl in Rye, New York. Later on in this book we will tell you how to make a mini-hothouse to speed up seed germination.

This peekaboo seed germinator was made from a paper cup. You can use milk cartons or paper cups whichever are available.

3. EXPERIMENT

A classic experiment shows how plants absorb water through their roots. A carrot is used. It is the root section of that plant.

Needed: A carrot with an unbroken skin, a tall glass, a cork, a plastic soda straw, and some blue or purple food coloring.

Directions: Whittle a hole in the cork to fit the straw. In the top of the carrot cut a hole that fits the cork. Cut off the bottom tip of the carrot. Mix a small quantity of sugar and water, as much sugar as the water will take up, and pour this into the hole in the carrot. Then insert cork and straw. Set the carrot in the glass, fill the glass with water to which the food coloring has been added, and set it aside.

Examine it after a few hours. Notice that the colored fluid has risen in the plastic straw. Remove the carrot and cut it lengthwise. You will see how the carrot absorbed and distributed the water. When you show this experiment, explain that this is a carrot osmometer—a device that measures the diffusion of a liquid.

Some of the experiments given later in the book take several days or weeks to complete and are tagged long-term experiments. Others can be done quickly, while you wait for a longer experiment to work out. Some of the activities described take only an hour or so.

You may want to include a hand lens in your equipment, to examine plants you are working with and to use in some activities. You may already have a microscope, or you may want to put one on a Christmas or birthday list. An adequate microscope can be purchased for several dollars. Here is an experiment that will let you see what may be done with a microscope.

4. EXPERIMENT

Here you observe what happens among one-celled plants and animals in your own water jungle.

Needed: A small amount of hay, a strainer, a glass jar, and a microscope slide. (If you live in the city and cannot get hay, possible substitutes are dried grass that is tall enough to show some seeds, or the straw used by stores to pack shipments of china.)

Directions: Make some hay tea by boiling the hay in water. Strain out the hay, and when the tea you have made is partially cooled, put it in a glass jar. Let the tea wait for two days. Then place a large drop of it on your slide, and look at it through the microscope.

You will find that one-celled organisms, both plant and animal, are in this hay tea. Watch the animals swim around your water jungle. After a period of time, new animals will arrive on the scene. Finally you will see the "tigers" of your jungle—Rotifera—arrive and devour everything else.

Sending Plants to School

You can teach plants to do new, unexpected things. You can have a plant contortionist, for example, or you can persuade a plant to bend down in a curve.

You can use plants from the garden or a local store, or you can raise a large supply of seedlings from one package of seeds. Small pots for the seedlings can be made from tin cans with holes in the bottom for drainage. Here is a sampling of experiments.

5. EXPERIMENT

A quick experiment shows how to make a plant bend down by giving it directed light.

Needed: A seedling two to three weeks old, and a source of light such as a small table lamp.

Directions: Place the light at one side of, and lower than, the plant. You can use a sheet of glass on which to stand the plant in its pot. Or put the plant very near the edge of a table or crate, with the lamp on the floor. The plant and lamp should be placed in the cellar or a closet, so the only light will come from the lamp.

By the next day the plant will be bending down toward its only source of light. Continue until the plant is well curved down.

6. EXPERIMENT

Making a plant turn into a contortionist is a long-term experiment. This also shows the plant's "determination" to turn toward light.

Needed: A long cardboard box at least a foot and a half long and two feet high, and a quick-growing young vine such as a garden pea.

Directions: Cut window holes in the box and its lid, as shown in the illustration. The position of these holes is important. Cut two cardboard partitions, about two-thirds the height of the box, and wedge them sideways across the box as illustrated. Place the vine in its pot in the left-hand section of the box. Make covers for the windows with pieces of cardboard cut a little larger than the window holes. Leave the window above the plant open and cover all the others, fastening the covers down flat with scotch tape, and turning over the ends of the tape so you can use them later as handles. Make sure the lid of the box fits on tightly,

WINDOW   WINDOW

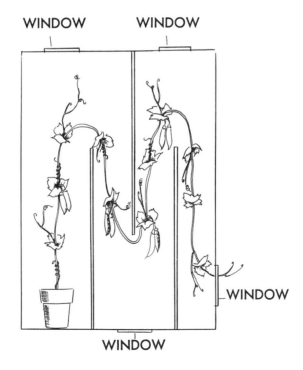

WINDOW

WINDOW

taping it if necessary, so that the plant is in the dark except for the window above toward which it will reach and climb. Set the box in sunlight and check the plant daily to see that the soil is moist.

You will see the plant climb toward the light coming through the window above it. When the plant has grown above the top of the nearest partition, close the window above it with one of the cardboard covers. Open the window at the lower side of the box and turn the box so this window faces the sunlight. Again make sure no other light enters the box. The vine will now curve over the partition and turn down toward the low open window.

When the plant has grown down near this window, close it. Take the cover off the other high window. Now the plant will slowly turn up again. When it reaches above the second partition, close this window and open the one in the end of the box. Now the plant will climb over this partition and turn down toward the end of the box.

Then remove the lid of the box so you can have a clear view of the plant. It will curve up and down, with a contortion like the waves of a roller coaster.

If you want a side view, tape the partitions to the bottom of the box with wide angles of scotch tape, and cut down two side corners of the box so the side can be let down.

7. EXPERIMENT

It is easy to change some plants into dwarfs or giants. Not all plants respond but you may enjoy experimenting with others besides those listed here. Since certain chemicals are not ordinarily used by children, ask your parents to help you with this experiment. Your local florist or hardware store will carry combinations of these chemicals under trade names.

Use Amo 1618 and B-Nine to *dwarf* chrysanthemums.

Cycocel will dwarf poinsettias.

Phosphon will retard the growth of petunias and chrysanthemums. Besides producing short-stemmed mums, Phosphon will delay the blooming of some varieties. Phosphon is to be used only by adults.

Gibberellic (Gibrel) will *increase* the growth and size of growing coleus, sedium, ivy, and ageratum. Gibrel will cause earlier blooming of petunias, asters, and pansies. It will make roses develop longer stems, geraniums larger flowers, and African violets more flowers. Many plants that ordinarily grow close to the ground and have short stems will show a spurt in growth. Gibrel should be used sparingly as directed and only by adults.

Wonder-brel is another growth stimulant, and geraniums, African violets, and gloxinia are among some plants that respond to it.

It is important to use young growing plants for these experiments. Be sure to follow the directions given.

Needed: The chemical growth stimulants and growth retardants named above. For each experiment, two young plants that are about the same size. It is better to have three plants, as one plant occasionally dies.

Directions: Give one plant the growth stimulator; give only water to the matching plant(s), which will be your control and will show normal growth without the influence of special chemicals. Since each of these plants will have identical growth conditions *except* for the chemical added to the treated plant, the untreated plant(s) will clearly show the different results.

In the same way, for your second set of plants, give one of the young plants the chemical to dwarf it and give the control plants water only. Be sure to give an equal amount of water to all of the plants, including the treated plants, in each experiment. You might wish to test the reactions of other young plants in addition to the plants mentioned above. Always use a control to check your results.

As your plants grow, you will see an effective contrast in sizes. If you find a type of plant that responds to both chemicals, you will have an interesting trio—dwarf, control, and giant.

While you are putting your mark on plants, why not have some tomatoes with your initials on them? Or you could use the initials of different members of your family.

8. EXPERIMENT

Tomatoes with initials on them make an amusing decoration for the dining table and show the effect of direct sunlight.

Needed: Several tomatoes that are entirely green, and aluminum foil.

Directions: Cut sections of foil large enough to wrap around each tomato, double thickness. Holding the double foil flat against a piece of cardboard, cut your initials or one large initial with a knife. The finished initials will show as openings in the foil. They should be wide enough to be clear. Wrap the tomatoes in pieces of foil, making sure that the openings of the initials are pressed smoothly and tightly against the tomato. Now all the light that can get to the tomato will be through the initials. Put the tomatoes in direct sunlight, initial side up. Keep one tomato unwrapped to serve as a color-timer.

When the color-timing tomato has turned red in sunlight, unwrap one tomato and make sure that the skin exposed through the cutout initials is red enough to show well. Let the tomatoes be exposed to sunlight until the initials show clearly on the tomato skin.

To make a plant go around a corner, showing its reaction to gravity, to build a plant maze for the plant to wander through, and for many other experiments in teaching plants to do new things, look through the many experiments in this book. And while you are deciding which experiment to do, have some seedlings growing.

Making Homes for Plants

If you build a hotbed for seeds and seedlings, you can start them growing early so they can be moved outdoors when the weather is warm enough. Also, with a hotbed you can hurry along seedlings for your experiments.

9. ACTIVITY

A large hotbed with good height can be used for both seedlings and seeds. You can make a simple one or one that is better insulated.

Needed: Get a strong cardboard box or carton from a store. The size will depend on the size of your ambition. Don't get a box smaller than four feet long by two feet wide by three feet high.

Directions: A hotbed with a slanting top is easier to work with, as it will admit more sunlight. At each front corner cut downward two feet. Now cut the sides at a slant. Then cut horizontally to remove this top two-foot section. The front will now be about one foot high, and the lid will cover the box at an angle. Cut a window in the lid. Around your window leave a two-inch margin to which you can fasten plastic with masking tape.

Paint the outside of the box black to absorb more heat energy from the sun. This will increase the temperature inside the box. Line the inside of the box with aluminum foil. For a warmer, better-insulated hotbed, use two cardboard boxes—one several inches larger than the other. Place the smaller box inside the larger box and fill the space between them, at the bottom as well as the sides, with sawdust, newspaper, or Styrofoam sheets.

Place a thermometer inside the hotbed so you can check and record the temperature. Also put in a dish filled with water to keep up humidity.

There will be room in the hotbed for pans in which seeds are planted and for seedlings in pots. This is also a good place to keep a plant while it waits to be used in an experiment.

Containers for seeds may be plastic pans from the hardware store or deep cake pans. Make some small holes to avoid rot. Putting a layer of small drainage pebbles at the bottom will also help prevent rot. Then add soil from the garden or bought by the bag. Smooth the top of the soil and plant your seeds at the depth directed on the package. Sprinkle them once a day with the kind of bottle and plunger spray used for window cleaning, if the soil feels dry. You will remember how the beans

A variety of "no cost" hot beds made by young scientists for experiments.

in Experiment 1 reacted to water, so do not let the soil get dry. Do not drown them, however, as some seeds can have too much water. You will find that seeds in the hotbed need less water than seeds planted outside. Soil should be moist but not soggy.

Make sure the containers of seeds are directly under the large window in the lid, and keep the hotbed in a place where it will get sunlight daily on the window.

A cheap, quickly made hotbed for seed germination will give you more space for different kinds of seeds. Also, you can start seeds there, while you are making a large hotbed. A small seedling hotbed can be easily made from two Styrofoam coffee cups. Cut half an inch off of the top of one cup so that it will fit upside down into the other container. In this cut-down cup cut a window. Leave a margin of half an inch at the top part. Make the window about an inch and a half wide and an inch high. Cover this window with Saran Wrap, using scotch tape to secure it. Add soil to the other cup after first making some small drainage holes in the bottom. Add a few pebbles and then the soil. Plant your seeds just under the top layer of soil. Put over it the cup with the window and you will have a mini-hotbed. Be sure to keep the soil moist.

10. ACTIVITY

This hotbed for seed germination is made from an egg carton. The compartments can be used to keep different kinds of seeds separated.

Directions: Use the kind of egg carton that resembles papier-mâché, with sides that feel thick in your fingers. Cut a wide window in the lid and cover with plastic or Saran Wrap, taped on. Punch a small hole for drainage in the bottom of each compartment. Line each compartment with aluminum foil in which you have punched several holes at the bottom. Fill the compartments with soil and plant the seeds. Set a tray or platter to catch water draining through.

A terrarium with glass sides and top is useful for many things. The plants inside can be easily seen. Some plants need its humid air. Carnivorous, or meat-eating, plants, for example, should have a terrarium. Plants in a terrarium need less frequent watering and can be safely left when you go away for a few days. Here are two terrariums to make—a large and a smaller one.

11. ACTIVITY

A terrarium can be made by using a shallow, well-calked box, with sides and top of glass panes cut at the hardware store to measure and taped at the corners with the top pane taped on all sides. But there is a simpler way to acquire such a terrarium.

Directions: Inquire at a pet shop for a "leaker"—an aquarium that leaks water and so cannot be used for fish. These are often sold cheaply. Spread epoxy glue, according to its directions, on the inside and outside of the aquarium bottom and on the inside of the corners for a third of the way up from the bottom. Put a layer of drainage pebbles on the bottom, mixed with charcoal that you have crushed with a hammer. Then put in at least three inches of soil.

Measure the top and have a piece of glass cut half an inch larger all around. Tape the edges before they start cutting any fingers. This cover will stay partly on all the time, with at least an inch open for fresh air.

12.   ACTIVITY

Making a smaller terrarium from a large-mouthed gallon jar.

Needed: A wide-mouthed gallon jar with its cover, plaster of paris or sand, and a large saucer for the jar to be placed on.

Directions: Wash the jar thoroughly. Prepare the plaster of paris as directed on the package and set the jar on its side pressed into the plaster of paris in the saucer. Plaster of paris hardens quickly. Press the jar lengthwise into the plaster to make a seat for the jar. Remove the jar before the plaster hardens, as you will want to be able to remove it from its seat from time to time. Use enough plaster of paris to heap it above the saucer's edge. This will give the jar a broader trough in which to sit. Sand may be used in place of plaster of paris, but it will not hold the jar as well. Prepare the inside as described earlier in "11. Activity." Punch several holes in the jar cover to provide a flow of air.

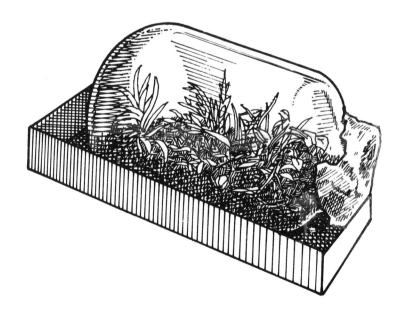

Carnivorous plants have different interesting ways of catching insects. Like some of the other plants mentioned in this book that are hard to find nearby, they can be ordered by mail from the address given at the back of the book.

Most of the activities and experiments given here are with young plants or seedlings. You can grow these cheaply and quickly and provide yourself with an ample supply of plants to work with. If you cannot find the seeds you want at a garden center or the many stores that display them, order them from the address in the Appendix.

Seedlings can also be bought at a nursery. If you want to start experiments quickly without spending any money, find someone with a garden that needs weeding and weed a flower bed in return for some seedlings.

If you live in a city apartment, arrange with the family to have first claim on a sunny window. You can use a wide shelf here or a table covered with a plastic sheet to protect it. This will be the center for the hotbed, for open window boxes of plants, for a terrarium, or for seeds and seedlings in pots.

These are all at-home activities and experiments that you can do alone or with the family or with friends. Some are projects you may want to take to school when they are finished, to show in class or for extra credit.

At school you may learn about further experiments and activities in the area of science that covers growing things. In the following section, some of the work done at one school is described. Here you will find more projects that can be done at home or school, and as you look through them you can note the ones that interest you.

SECTION II

In the following pages are a variety of experiments and activities for you to choose from. These form part of a pilot program in the new science, carried out for several years by Mark Fleitzer, head of science for the sixth grades and science resource teacher for Midland School, Rye, New York.

These projects, like those in the first section, are a mixture of old and new. They include classic experiments that have come down to us through the years, adaptations of older experiments, experiments that originated with Charles Darwin, and new activities and experiments developed by Mark Fleitzer and his students. They are divided according to the time needed to set them up and do them—into short-, medium-, and long-term projects. They are given here with added details for home use.

Short-term Experiments and Activities

Projects in this group will either be completed rapidly or show quick results. For these and the following projects, a record should be kept.

Records are an important part of all scientific work, will be interesting to read over later, and are useful in describing home projects in the classroom. It is important to make the notes as things happen so as not to lose the freshness of your observations. Notes can be taken on pages to be placed in a loose-leaf notebook; they can be left as made during the experiment or copied for a more formal appearance. Sketches are often useful.

Precision is important for these records. The exact amount of seeds and other materials used, the time when results of the experiment started to show, any interesting points in the progress of experiment or activity all should be noted. The last part of each report should tell what the experiment proved or why an activity can be valuable.

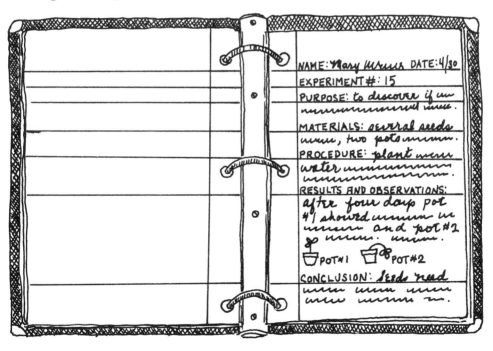

13. EXPERIMENT

Growing seeds on an ordinary plastic sponge that is kept moist will give you a crop that looks like thick green bristles of a brush. This will show growth without special nutrients. You can also show the incomplete manufacture of chlorophyll in the absence of light, by doing a companion experiment in which you keep a second sponge with its seeds in a box or closet where it will get no light. Details about chlorophyll will be found in later experiments, which need more time, as well as the experience you will gain through short-term projects.

Needed: A small amount of grass seed, and a sponge with or without an indentation at the top. For variations in the experiment, four sponges and more grass seed will be needed.

Directions: Place the moistened sponge in a deep saucer or plastic dish with a rim. Scatter seed thickly and evenly on top. Water daily, with a window-cleaning type of plunger and bottle, or by pouring water on the sponge very gently so the seeds will not pile up on top of each

Lush growth from seeds placed in a sponge.

other. There should only be enough water added to drain down to a small amount in the saucer. The sponge garden should be placed where it will get regular sunlight.

For a comparison set of sponge gardens, start a second one three days after the first; a third one three days later. Some authorities suggest using bird seed, and you might want to do this for the third sponge garden, to give variety.

For the companion experiment to show that the grass plants can not make chlorophyll in darkness and that a lack of chlorophyll affects the plants, place the fourth sponge and seeds in a closet or covered carton. Check it daily for moisture. Be sure to do this in very dim light.

The seeds will sprout rapidly, and you can then watch the development of the stems and the blades, or leaves. Note how the sponge distributes water evenly, without rot, and the way roots find small holes in the sponge. Watch the different appearance of the sponge garden you have kept in darkness and note the results in your record. The spindly growth in darkness is due to the stem cells stretching lengthwise. Plants produce growth regulators. In this case the absence of light and the substance that regulates cell growth allow the stem cells to fill with water and stretch.

In the record mention the contrasting appearance of a sponge garden that grew in the light. You may wish to try growing one sponge garden in the dark for a longer time. See what eventually happpens to these seedlings. The green color in plants is due to a pigment called chlorophyll. Only plants that have chlorophyll can make food. In a later experiment you can remove chlorophyll from a plant.

Chlorophyll is the name for the green pigments in plants. Chlorophyll in plants captures light energy, and together with carbon dioxide and water, it makes food which the plant stores. An energy transfer takes place as light energy is changed into chemical energy. Not all plants contain the chlorophylls, and not all living things that contain chlorophyll are plants.

14. ACTIVITY

This project shows the effect of acids working on minerals in the soil. The action of acids on minerals is illustrated clearly and dramatically by placing an egg in a glass of vinegar and observing the results.

You will see that the eggshell is slowly dissolved by the acid vinegar. Minerals in the eggshell are dissolved and ready to be distributed by the liquid. In your report explain that in this manner minerals in the soil are dissolved by acids in the soil with the help of soil water. These minerals in liquid form are then spread through the soil, taken up by plants, and obtained by people from food plants.

15. EXPERIMENT

This is a project to demonstrate that a plant grows faster in soda water, which provides extra carbon dioxide.

Needed: Four glasses, two slightly smaller than the others, and all of them slanting out slightly toward the top. This shape of glass is commonly found in many stores. Also needed are two small plants or seedlings of the same kind and size you have grown in your hotbed.

Directions: Put a layer of small pebbles at the bottom of the two larger glasses and cover them with at least two inches of soil. Carefully transplant into the soil two seedlings or small plants. Cover with the smaller glasses, to form small greenhouse roofs. Water one plant, your control, with plant water. In any experiment, the control is an example of normal conditions in contrast to the special condition being tested. Water the test plant in the other glass with soda water only. Each day, continue to add plain water to the control plant and soda water to the test plant, until liquid begins to reach the drainage pebbles at the bottom. Label the glass containing the test plant or put a twig in the soil beside it so you will be sure that the right plant gets the daily soda water. Compare the differences between the two plants as they grow.

In your report, note the importance to the plant of the carbon dioxide released from the soda water. List as many points as you can see, such as increased growth, faster growth, and strength, as compared to the control plant that got only plain water.

A charcoal briquette crystal garden in bloom.

16. ACTIVITY

A crystal garden is attractive in the house and amusing to show your friends. It illustrates the process of osmosis, and you can note the distribution of water as the crystals grow. Be sure to add water carefully and slowly as needed.

Needed: Here again the diplomatic work you have put in, interesting your family in your projects, will pay off in helpful offers of materials. You will need as many charcoal briquettes as will fit neatly into the bottom of a glass bowl. You will also need one-quarter cup of laundry bluing, one-quarter cup salt, and one tablespoon of household ammonia. An inexpensive, shallow glass bowl or a pyrex cooking dish will make the container.

Directions: Arrange the charcoal briquettes in the bottom of the container and partly cover them with a mixture of the bluing, salt, and ammonia, together with one-quarter cup of water. If you want colors in your garden, put a drop of colored ink or food coloring on two or three pieces of charcoal. You can make a comparison test if you can obtain bituminous or soft coal. Use it in a separate bowl and follow the same directions.

Within a few days crystals should be well formed. You will soon have a dramatic crystal garden. The record can state when the first crystals showed, how they developed, and can describe the final effect. Distribution of water can be noted. You might add the guesses of your friends about what surprising new thing you are growing.

31

17.   EXPERIMENT

This is an experiment to show how roots will find their way around an obstacle that blocks their path.

Needed: A seedling such as a very young sunflower, a container such as a flowerpot or a box lined with plastic so it will be watertight, and a piece of wood about four inches long and an inch across.

Directions: Plant the seedling in the container, about half an inch above the piece of wood. Settle the wood firmly, so it will make a barrier as the roots go down. Give the plant a few days, and then carefully brush aside enough soil so you can see that the roots are beginning to find their way around the wood and are turning down again. Carefully replace the soil, pressing it gently. Check again in a few more days. When the roots have finally turned completely around the wood and reach below it, draw a sketch of the strangely shaped roots for your report.

If you want to do your own personal experiment, try a plant in some soil in a large glass jar. For good results, you will have to estimate the best position for the plant with its roots and the wood near enough the side of the jar so you can see the roots making their turn. There must be a strip of cardboard held around the jar with masking tape because the roots need darkness. You can remove this briefly at intervals to see how the roots are doing. Keep a careful record of how you place the plant and wood, how long it takes for the root system to reach the wood, turn around it, and resume its normal direction downward.

18. EXPERIMENT

The stem of a plant also will make its way around a barrier and continue its upward growth. This experiment shows what happens.

Needed: A shallow wooden box filled with soil, a wooden slat, and half a dozen seedlings that are just breaking through the earth.

Directions: Transplant the seedlings into the box, in a line across it. Nail the slat across the box, directly above the seedlings. Make sure that the soil is high enough so the tops of the seedlings almost touch the slat. Water daily. The seedlings would normally grow straight up, but now the barrier of wood is above them.

In a very few days you will see the tips of the seedlings growing around the slat. The stems turn under the wood, continue under it, and then turn up against the side of the slat where they are free to rise.

19. EXPERIMENT

Do seeds need air to germinate? This experiment will tell you.

Needed: Two small pill bottles with caps, three packages of flower seeds.

Directions: Wash the pill bottles thoroughly. Boil a cup of water for five minutes and let it cool. Put about a dozen seeds, mixed from the packages, in each bottle. Fill one bottle to the top with the boiled water. Fill the other bottle with tap water. This is the control bottle. Label this bottle. Watch what happens to the seeds in the two jars. Will the seeds sprout in the boiled water, which contains less air?

20. EXPERIMENT

This experiment illustrates that water must get inside the seed before it can sprout.

Needed: Dried beans or peas, a large dish or pan, a candle, a sieve, and some pieces of clean cloth such as an old bath towel or several layers of thinner cloth folded together to fit the dish.

Directions: Use a dozen bean or pea seeds. Coat six of them thoroughly with melted wax. You can place them on a piece of cardboard and drip melted wax on them from the lighted candle. Soak these six seeds and the six control seeds without the wax in the dish filled with water, for about ten hours. Drain them carefully in the sieve, slowly so the wax will not crack off. At this point, note the difference between the appearance of the seeds with wax and of those without wax, and put this down in the record. Then place the dozen seeds between folds of cloth in the dish. If a thick cloth is used, one layer over and one under is enough. Dampen the cloth with mildly warm water. Keep the seeds moist until sprouts appear.

Which seeds are sprouting? What has happened to the six seeds with a wax coating? Note in your report that water often enters some seeds through a tiny opening in the seed coat(s) or through nicks or scratches in the seed coat(s). Water seems to be the only thing needed for most seeds to grow, although some seeds need special conditions to complete their growth as seeds. Later in this book an activity will tell you how to use seed-coat swelling and shrinking to make unusual beads.

21. EXPERIMENT

This experiment shows exactly how the leaves of a plant turn to face the sun. The tendency of plants to do this is called heliotropism.

Needed: One geranium plant, and a sunny day.

Directions: Select one leaf of the plant for your experiment. Note for your record the position of this leaf in relation to the sun. Make a drawing—a simple diagram—of the plant as seen from above. Draw an arrow to show the direction of the sunlight toward your experimental leaf. Every hour, for at least five hours, record how the position of the leaf changes. Draw diagrams showing each new change in the position of the leaf, and each new angle of the sun toward the leaf.

At the end of this time, the leaf will have turned around to follow the sun. You will have a series of drawings showing movement, in slow motion, caught each hour. Your record will give a detailed description of the way the leaf turned. The geranium is only one of the plants that exhibit heliotropism. You may find other plants which have leaves that notably turn to follow the sun, and you might describe them in your report.

22. EXPERIMENT

Charles Darwin, the great English naturalist, studied the effects of gravitation on plants. In one of his books Darwin tells about the work of another plant investigator, Andrew Knight, who nearly fifty years earlier had experimented with young seedlings. Knight was very interested in how gravity affected germinating seeds. He tried growing seedlings on the side of a waterwheel. He found that centrifugal force, the force away from the center of the turning wheel, acted like gravity. Knight was not sure whether this force overcame gravity or replaced gravity's force. The seedlings grew in a different manner when on the revolving waterwheel.

You may use a record player for this experiment. Run it for two to three days at 45 or 78 revolutions per minute. Or you may enjoy making the necessary equipment, using a small electric motor, easily obtained from a local store for nothing, and a few pieces of cardboard. Many stores have revolving signs in their front window. Ask a friendly store owner for such a display sign. Try to get one that is a circle of cardboard about thirty inches in diameter. Be sure to ask the store owner ahead of time, and tell him why you want the sign. These signs are usually powered by a six-volt battery. The motor should revolve at about fifty revolutions per minute. On many motors the motor speed will double if you double the voltage. Do this by adding one more six-volt battery in series connection.

Needed: Six or eight paper cups large enough to hold several seedlings that are about one to two inches tall and are long-stemmed plants; some small pebbles for drainage, enough for each cup; some masking tape; soil.

Directions: Fill each paper cup with soil until it is three-fourths full. Carefully transplant into each cup a half-dozen seedlings from your hotbed. Fill the cups to the top with soil. Cut some two-inch-long pieces of masking tape. Split each piece lengthwise into at least three strips. Wait a few days until the seedlings are doing nicely. Remove the weaker plants from each cup. Carefully crisscross some of these strips of

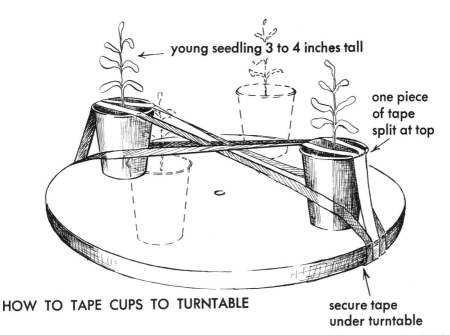

young seedling 3 to 4 inches tall

one piece
of tape
split at top

HOW TO TAPE CUPS TO TURNTABLE

secure tape
under turntable

masking tape over the top of each cup, being careful not to touch the stems of the seedlings. Leave small openings between the strips so you can water each plant every other day. Fasten the ends of the strips to the sides of the cups. The masking tape strips will prevent the soil from falling out when the cups are revolving, and will retard evaporation. Add just enough water to keep the soil moist.

Using masking tape, fasten each cup to the outside of the revolving circular piece of cardboard or to the record player turntable. Be sure to tell your parents about this experiment, as you will need their cooperation. The plants should be in a room with light coming from several directions. The plants and the equipment should not be touched for three to four days. Allow the motor to run day and night for this time, but be sure to stop the motor when watering the plants. After this period of time you will see some surprising results. For additional fun, carefully tear away the paper cups and examine the roots and their growth. At a slower speed of rotation, the desired effects are much less apparent and will take longer to show up.

23. EXPERIMENT

The value of a hotbed is illustrated by this experiment.

Needed: A dozen seeds of quick-growing flowers such as zinnia or marigold, two flowerpots, and a sheet of glass or plastic that will cover one pot.

Directions: In one flowerpot plant six seeds at the depth indicated on the seed package. Water the soil so the seeds will be thoroughly soaked and be sure the soil is not too tightly packed for good drainage. This will be the control. Plant six seeds in the other pot in the same way and water them, but cover this pot. If you use glass for a cover, tape the edges so they will not cut or scrape your hands. If you use plastic, fit it firmly around the top of the pot so it makes a tight cover; you can fasten it with scotch tape, folding the ends of the tape over several times to make handles that you can use to take off the tape and plastic easily for daily watering. Place the two pots in sunlight. You will soon see moisture forming on the underside of the glass or plastic. When you lift the cover to water the plants, the air in the covered pot will be damp and warm. Leave the cover off for a few minutes when watering, so the air will freshen.

Compare the way the seedlings grow in the two pots, which received an equal amount of light and water. There have been differences in humidity and temperature. The covered pot has also had some air restriction.

The next six experiments will be tests for nutrients in seeds, plants, and foods that we get from plants. By these experiments we can find out where some of our important food elements come from.

Some of the experiments are easy and done with materials found in the home. Some require your close attention and for some you will need to make purchases at the drugstore. So read all six before you decide which experiment to do first.

24. EXPERIMENT

Starches or carbohydrates are nutrients or food materials. This experiment is a test for starch.

Needed: Half a dozen potatoes, a section of thin cloth, several filter papers such as those used for coffee, a grater, iodine, and a bowl.

Directions: Grate several potatoes, put the pulp in the cloth, and pull the corners of the cloth together to form a bag. Hold the bag in the bowl carefully so the pulp stays inside, add a little water, and then kneed and press the bag until milky liquid shows in the bowl. This is easier to see if the bowl is glass. Shape a piece of filter paper into a funnel, with the bottom closed, and slowly pour the liquid through it into a glass. After the water has drained through the filter paper, the paper will be well saturated with starch from the potatoes. Allow the filter paper to dry, then prove the starch content by placing a drop of iodine on the filter paper. Tincture of iodine is a sure test for the presence of starch.

The color change you see proves the presence of starch in the potatoes. Cornstarch declares what it is by its name. Test cornstarch for a companion experiment. You might also try testing other starchy foods such as cooked spaghetti. Use jelly glasses. Into one pour a mixture of cornstarch and water, into the second put your potato liquid unstrained, and into the third put some cooked spaghetti ground up with some water. At the same time you might also try testing the water rice has been cooked in or that macaroni has been boiled in, adding some water to each of the last two samples. Have one glass with plain water for a control. To each glass add a few drops of iodine with a clean eyedropper. Observe the results, and then write them down for your report.

For a final note for your record of your tests of foods and household materials for starch, mix an equal number of drops of iodine and water, pour a little of this solution on a freshly cut slice of potato, and describe the results.

In the next experiment you can find out if leaves contain starch.

25. EXPERIMENT

To test leaves for starch content, they should be picked after the sun has been on them for some hours. In order to see the color change indicator iodine work, it is first necessary to remove the plant pigmentation that colors the leaves. Otherwise this coloration will mask our results.

Needed: Some acetone solvent from the drugstore. Be careful with this because it is an inflammable solvent that evaporates quickly into the air around it. Do not use it in the kitchen for this reason. Some leaves are needed for testing. Select several geranium leaves that have been in strong sunlight for about half the day. You might also try some other leaves such as vegetable plant leaves—bean, tomato, or lettuce. Try a few tree leaves such as sugar maple or birch. Try some broad-leaf shrubs, but avoid those with heavy waxy leaves.

Directions: Place the leaves in vigorously boiling water for a few minutes. This helps to extract the pigmentation. Remove the leaves and place them in a bowl to which you add the acetone. The chlorophyll will seep out slowly so knead the leaves gently to speed up the process. It is possible to use an eggbeater, but this tends to break the leaves into very small pieces. After the leaves or their fragments become whitish, place them on paper toweling to dry. Drop some iodine on each fragment. If you used the first method and your leaves are whole, take a knife and crosshatch the leaf to help the iodine seep into the cells where the starch grains are. After a few minutes you will see the characteristic color appear in those places, showing that starch is present.

It is also possible to test leaves for glucose sugar. In the next experiment you will need Clinistix, which you can get at any drugstore. These plastic strips contain a test area at the end of each strip.

26. EXPERIMENT

To see how these Clinistix test strips work, it is a good idea to try them out on a few household items first. The test kit contains a color chart that matches colors to amounts of sugar. In this case the sugar is glucose, a simple sugar. For dramatic results, try several brown sugars, such as free-pouring brown sugar or light-brown cane sugar, and some diluted honey. Add some water to a small spoonful of honey to dilute it. Put one of the test strips under the water faucet for a comparison control. In using these strips, be sure to immerse them very briefly in each liquid being tested and to shake off the excess. Full directions are included in the kit. Be sure to mix the brown sugars with some water before you test them.

Needed: The Clinistix kit mentioned, the brown sugars mentioned, a few other items you may wish to test such as jelly or jam, and some leaves.

Directions: Gather a collection of leaves from different plants. Be sure to gather three or four leaves from each plant, or more if the leaves are small. Be sure to include some of the grasses such as the leaves of wheat, corn, oats, and barley if you can obtain them. Try some of the common grass clippings from your lawn, including some of the weed grasses.

Chop each type of leaf separately. Grind each with some fine sand in a pyrex custard cup. Use a heavy stick. As you grind, add water until you have a heavy paste. Strain through a fine cloth. Test each sample separately. Be sure to dip the test strip into each just briefly and wait ten seconds for the results.

27. EXPERIMENT

Here are two methods to test for the presence of acid in foods.

Needed: Litmus paper, which is paper soaked in a vegetable dye made from lichen. It can be purchased locally and if possible, get all blue litmus paper. Also needed are a lemon, a little sour milk, grape juice, and vinegar.

Directions: In the first method, dip the litmus paper in vinegar and note the result. Then use the litmus paper to test lemon juice and sour milk for acid. In the second method, add a teaspoon of grape juice to half a glass of water. Now add half a teaspoon of lemon juice or vinegar to the grape juice mixture and record the resulting color.

Blue litmus paper serves as an indicator of acid by turning red when acid is present. Some fruits serve as indicators also; this is true of grapes, and thus the grape juice indicates the presence of acid. Purple cabbage, crushed into a pulp, also serves as an indicator.

28.   EXPERIMENT

In this experiment you will isolate gluten, which is a protein found in wheat flour. Protein is needed for the growth and repair of our bodies. Much protein is present in meats and dairy products. It is also manufactured in our bodies from amino acids, the building blocks of our body chemistry. You will also apply the starch test to the material you separate from the gluten.

Needed: A pint of wheat flour, a cloth bag or a large piece of cloth, and iodine.

Directions: Mix the flour in a bowl with enough water to make a stiff paste. Knead the paste, pressing it together pushing it down flat, piling it up and pressing it again. After kneading for several minutes, adding a sprinkling of flour if the paste is too sticky, put it in the bag or in the cloth drawn together in the shape of a bag. Knead the bag of paste underwater in a bowl. Keep the first milky liquid for later testing. Then continue rinsing. The easiest way to do this is under a running faucet. Otherwise, use the bowl after pouring the first rinsing liquid into a jar; continue changing the water until the milky look disappears. Open the bag and examine the sticky mass, which is gluten.

Take the first rinsing water with the milky appearance that you saved. Add a few drops of iodine and note how soon the color of the liquid changes. What does its new color prove is present in the liquid?

29. ACTIVITY

In this activity you will draw diagrams of simple flowers to show their circular arrangement.

Needed: As many simple flowers as you can find that do not have a disk of small florets in the center (such as buttercups and petunias).

Directions: Inspect the first flower. Note the sepals making up the outer circle. Note their color. Next come the petals, inside the sepals. Remove the petals after noting for your drawing their position in respect to the sepals. This will allow you to examine the rest of the flower more easily. Next come the stamens, a ring of little knobs, each on a stalk. In the center you will see the pistil. Make your drawing, one circle inside another, with a dotted line going out from each of the four parts to their names that you can write at the side of the diagram. Do several flowers, noting for each any differences such as the number of petals. Both the sepals and the petals are leaves. Can you find flowers with the petals each separated from one another? Or with the petals joined together near the stalk?

30. ACTIVITY

This activity is short but satisfying, and parents will approve your attack on a common lawn pest.

Purslane is a common and troublesome relation of rose moss that roots very easily. You can identify it from its picture on the colored charts of lawn pests distributed by grass seed companies.

Pull up a good supply of purslane from the lawn. Spread the plants out on a bare stretch of soil where you can observe them easily. Let them lie in the sun without water. The taproots will bend over, touch the soil, and begin growing. You will have an example of the plant's determination to go on growing.

31. ACTIVITY

Here is an attractive necklace, easily and cheaply made, that girls can wear or that boys can make to give to their mothers.

Needed: Enough navy marrow beans for a necklace of the desired length plus a dozen or so extra beans, some crochet thread and a needle with an eye large enough to accept the thread easily, some blue Tintex dye, and a pan in which to soak the beans.

Directions: Place the navy marrow beans in the pan and add enough water to cover them. Add one teaspoon of blue Tintex dye. Soak the beans at least twelve hours or until they are soft. String immediately. Some will sprout but you can remove them easily. As the seed coat shrinks, the blue pigmentation will tend to collect in its folds. The resulting multitudinous wrinkles give a beautiful natural patina of dark-blue, veinlike appearance. For a more attractive necklace, dye the thread also.

A hand lens will be needed for the next two activities.

32. ACTIVITY

Watermelon seeds are in two colors, black and white. Observe carefully the external differences in size. Take one white and one black seed and let them dry thoroughly. Remove the skin from each with a knife. Split the seeds in half, lengthwise. Examine the half seeds through your hand lens. Does each seed contain the embryo necessary for the growth of a new plant? Make a drawing for your report and note all the differences in each of the observed seeds. For an additional experiment, try planting some of the black seeds and some of the white seeds to see which grow.

33. ACTIVITY

The root hairs that grow from a seed absorb water·and take in dissolved minerals from the soil. If you start seeds growing on a sponge, they will not have any soil for minerals, but they can be easily seen without earth around them and their root hairs can be observed.

Use a saucer or dish with a raised rim. Place a wet sponge with one end on the rim and the other slanting down into the saucer. Half fill the saucer with water. The water will spread up the sponge as needed. Near the top of the sponge at the rim end, sprinkle a variety of small seeds, such as radish, and some seeds for canaries or parakeets. In a few days the seeds will sprout. They will sprout faster if you soak them overnight before placing them on the sponge. With the hand lens, you will see the tiny root hairs. Afterward you may want to plant the sprouting seeds for seedlings and radishes.

A microscope will be needed for the next experiment.

34.   EXPERIMENT

Cells of a plant that are filled with chlorophyll can be seen through a microscope and can be distinguished from other cells.

Needed: A moss plant or a stem of the plant, tweezers, and a microscope slide.

Directions: Using the tweezers, remove a single leaf from the moss plant or stem. The leaves are arranged spirally around the stem. Flatten this leaf out on the microscope slide and add a drop of water. Examine under the microscope. You will see cells with tiny green capsules filled with chlorophyll—the chloroplasts. These are the cells that use light energy to form foods, a process called photosynthesis.

You might try to see the cells containing chlorophyll in the leaves of another plant such as clover. But this will be more difficult, as leaves of higher plants are usually eight or more cells thick, and it is thus hard to distinguish the cells. Moss is chosen for this experiment because it has a simple structure, usually one cell thick, and the cells thus show up clearly under the microscope. Try two or three moss leaves, to get a clear pattern, before making a sketch for your record.

Medium-term Experiments and Activities

Medium-term projects take longer than those you have been doing but are not harder to work out. You will need to inspect some of these at intervals, to be sure plants have enough moisture, to check a special stage of progress, and to note interesting points for your reports.

Some of the experiments will carry on further the work you have done in the short-term projects. Some will open up new areas of plant testing and demonstration.

35. EXPERIMENT

This is an experiment developed at the New York Botanical Gardens. Keep a careful report, as you will be among the first young people to do it. It is an interesting way to test a plant's response to magnetism, gravity, and light. This type of response is called tropism.

Needed: A package of granular agar from any biological supply house near your area; a package of mustard seeds; a plastic sandwich box, which is square and shallow; a large horseshoe magnet, the three-pound size or the five-pound size. These are available from war surplus supply companies, one of which is listed at the back of the book.

Directions: Make an agar jelly, following the directions included with the nutrient agar package. Pour the mixture while it is still liquid into the bottom of the sandwich box until the box is half full. When the mixture has hardened to a tough jellylike state, cut out an oblong space with a knife, removing jelly carefully so you will have neat sides. The position of this oblong space is shown in the illustration; the strip of jelly remaining on the smaller side should not be too narrow. Put the top on the box, set it on edge, with the cut out space toward the top, and check the position with the illustration. If the lid makes the box rest unevenly, place strips of paper underneath the box until it is level. Take off the lid, observe the jelly, and you will see that the bottom of the cut out space makes a shelf of jelly. Sprinkle mustard seed on this shelf. Close the box again and keep it in the upright position. The seeds will germinate and grow into the jelly, without added water. When the seedlings are half an inch above the jelly shelf, you are ready to start three tests.

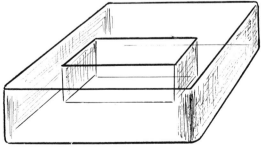

First you will test the plants' response to gravity. Turn the box so it rests on a side edge, instead of the bottom edge. The oblong space will now run up and down, and your seedlings will be reaching out sideways. For a few days watch the effects on the seedlings of this new position of the box. You will see them start to make a right-angle turn upward and their roots turn to grow down. As they respond to gravity in the new position, they will eventually make a pattern as shown in the second illustration—stems going up and roots going down.

You may do the next two tests with the same plants. But your results will be more clearly seen if you use three sandwich boxes set up with agar-jelly shelves and seeds in the same way, one for each test.

The second test shows the plants' response to light. Place the box so the plants get strong sunlight from one direction. Notice how the seedlings will bend toward the direction from which the light comes. Seedlings and older plants respond to light shining on them from one side by bending toward the source of light. This response is called phototropism.

For best results, avoid artificial light in this experiment, as this light will tend to interfere with your results. You can control artificial light in your testing area by placing the plastic box inside a small box. A shoe box will do nicely. You can place the cover on it at night to avoid moving the plastic box with the growing seedlings. If you hinge the lid with tape and tape both boxes in position, your results will be more satisfying.

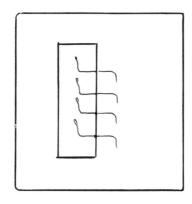

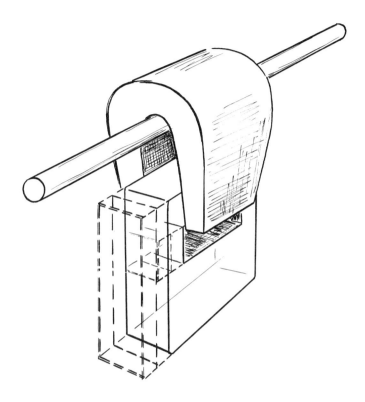

For the third test, arrange a wooden dowel or a strong cord above the box of agar jelly so that you can gradually move your horseshoe magnet along it. Be sure to use at least a half-inch dowel. If you fasten the ends of the dowel with tape to two boxes, also taped in place, the heavy magnet will be more easily moved along and with less chance of collapsing on the plastic box.

Start with the magnet in position, its two ends coming down across the narrow part of the box so that one pole of the magnet is on each side of the plants. Move the magnet slowly along the rod or cord, a fraction of an inch every half day. Watch the response of the plants and describe it in your report.

36. EXPERIMENT

Here you will find where leaf development starts on a stem. You will also observe any difference between cotyledons and true leaves.

Needed: Seedlings in different stages of growth from your hotbed.

Directions: Remove from the hotbed a small flowerpot that has been planted with seeds and in which the seedlings are appearing. Examine them and spend several days making drawings of the seedlings as they grow. Note that the leaf development is at the tip of the growing stem. Also note that the first leaves to appear on most of your plants are the cotyledons that have been curled ready in the seeds and now provide food for the plant. These early leaves wither and disappear as they are no longer needed and the true leaves appear. When a leaf is large enough to examine in detail, you will see the tiny veins that carry nutrient liquids.

37. ACTIVITY

Compound or composite flowers are really clusters of tiny flowers or florets. Composite flowers look like bouquets when you examine them closely. In this activity you will separate several kinds of composite flowers and draw, first the single floret, then a combination of florets showing how they fold together.

Some of the compound flowers are daisy, black-eyed Susan, aster, thistle, sunflower, and chrysanthemum. Take one of these flowers and very carefully pry apart its arrangement so you can pluck out some of the florets with tweezers. Notice that each floret is a separate flower with its own pistils and stamens that has been packed in together with other florets. After this, when you see a daisy, you may no longer think of it as a single flower but as a multiple flower or bouquet of florets.

38. EXPERIMENT

For a permanent exhibit of plant growth over a month's time, mount specimens on a large piece of poster board.

Needed: A dozen seeds of the same plant, a large flowerpot or waterproof box, poster board, Saran Wrap and quick-drying glue.

Directions: Plant the seeds, and if you are using a flowerpot, put it in your large hotbed for quicker growth. Check the seeds daily, taking up one and replacing it carefully, till a seed has started to germinate. As soon as activity shows, remove that seed and mount it on the poster board with glue. Three days later, carefully dig up another seed, which should be further along in growth, and mount it beside the first.

Continue removing the seeds and eventually the seedlings, at three-day intervals. You will find that by working slowly and brushing the soil carefully away from them, they will be in good condition to mount. One easy method is to use a teaspoon, scooping out a deep spoonful of earth together with the germinating seed and then blowing and brushing the soil away. If the soil is damp and clots, set the seed and soil aside so that the earth is dry before you start brushing. As the seedlings grow, dig deeper with the spoon so the roots won't be cut. Put the earth and seedling on a sheet of paper and work gently toward the part of the stem bearing the roots that is covered with soil. As your seedlings get larger, you may want to press them between sheets of blotting paper or several thicknesses of newspaper, before mounting them, so the plants will show well instead of drying in a tangled condition.

To preserve the root systems and the fragile stems and leaves, small pieces of Saran Wrap, kept unwrinkled, can be glued over each plant. In the end, you will have an effective exhibit of plant growth from seed to well-formed seedling.

39.   EXPERIMENT

An experiment that shows very clearly the process of seed germination is done with radish seeds in a glass jar.

Needed: Thirty radish seeds, and a glass jar.

Directions: Put the radish seeds in the jar and add about one and a half inches of water. Put the cover on the jar so the water will not evaporate. After two weeks the sprouting seeds will be ready for observation.

You will probably see some oil that the seeds have given off. The separated seed coats will lie apart on the bottom of the jar. The rootlets, the root hairs, and the growing embryo will all be clearly visible. In the drawings for your record, you may want to enlarge these two or three times.

When you have finished the descriptions and drawings for your record, take out the sprouting radish seeds and settle them in soil where they will grow.

40.   EXPERIMENT

As leaves of a plant carry on their growth activities, oxygen is formed. How does the gas leave the plant? This experiment will show you.

Needed: A plant leaf, a glass or dish, and some water.

Directions: Make sure that the leaf you are going to use has been in sunlight for several hours immediately before the experiment. Take the leaf off the plant just before you start. Add some water to the dish in which you have placed the leaf. Note the bubbles rising from the leaf as the gas escapes. They come from small openings in the leaf that are called stomata. Turn the leaf over, underwater, to observe both sides. You will probably notice there are more stomata on the bottom of the leaf. You will have a good action drawing of bubbles rising from the leaf for your report.

41. EXPERIMENT

This experiment shows that roots will grow toward a source of water.

Needed: A container or planter, which may be a plastic tray with a high rim, from the hardware store, or a flat tray for seedlings that you can get free from a nursery and line with plastic to make it waterproof. You will need seeds that will grow quickly and sturdily, such as marigold seeds. You may get seeds from a green-thumb friend or relative, or buy a package (about fifteen cents).

If you have set up a hotbed and started seeds, you probably have a watering pot with a fine-spray nozzle. Or you can make a spray device, for no cost, from a glass milk bottle with heavy foil across the top. Puncture tiny holes in the foil and fasten it on the bottle with rubber bands. You can also get a large plastic pepper shaker at a local store.

Directions: Put a one-inch layer of pebbles for drainage at the bottom of your planter. Add two to three inches of soil from the garden or from a florist or garden supply store. Plant several rows of seeds at the depth indicated on the package. Place in sunlight and water daily. In this experiment the main thing to remember is that you do all the watering across only one wide corner of the planter. Thus this section only will have really moist soil, and the rest of the soil will be progressively drier the farther away it is from the damp corner. You will notice the effect on the seeds.

After several weeks, remove the soil gradually and carefully from several seedlings that are beyond the damp corner. As you expose the roots of the seedlings, brushing earth away from them, you will see that the roots are growing toward the moist corner of the box. Water is vital to plants, and roots will grow in the direction of a supply of water and turn through the soil to reach it.

As you have seen, it is a good thing to have your own supply of seedlings ready for experiments. These may be in hotbeds or transplanted from hotbeds to planters and window boxes. To add to this supply of plants, you can have a variety of plants that you have grown by methods other than planting seeds. The next experiment tells how.

42. EXPERIMENT

Plants can be reproduced in various ways from parts of their structure. In this experiment, use at least two of the methods described below.

Needed: Several sturdy parent plants of the kinds suggested below, a potato, and a container for new planting.

Directions:

A. Reproduction from a cutting of part of a stem. You can experiment with many plants. Some of these are coleus, geranium, fuchsia, lemon verbena, and petunia. You can get a section of stem from a friend with a garden, or buy a plant at a nursery. The plant should not be so young that the stems are not strong. The geranium, for example, will produce strong new shoots in no more than three weeks that will have several leaves and will make good cuttings. Also, the plant from which you take your stem section should not be so old that it is tough and woody. Cut off your section of stem with a knife, at a slant. This section will contain the tip of that shoot or branching part of the plant. Take off leaves at the cut end, leaving four or five at the tip end. The container for your cuttings can be a flowerpot or waterproofed box. Drainage is important, so use the layer of pebbles at the bottom and mix a little sand with your soil. Insert the cut end of the section in the soil, with about half the section covered with earth. Firm the soil around the section. This cutting will do better if it is covered, either with a sheet of plastic supported by sticks or with a glass jar turned upside down. Remove the covering for ten minutes daily when you check to see if the soil is moist or needs watering. Do not place the cutting in sunlight.

If you want to do your own experiment with several cuttings from different plants, you might like to make a propagating box. At a hardware store, get a clear plastic box with a tight-fitting lid, the type of box used for a crisper in the refrigerator. Be sure to get a box made of stiff clear plastic, not the clouded soft kind. Use the layer of drainage pebbles. Instead of all-purpose soil, use a mixture of half milled peat moss and half builders' sand, which can be obtained at a garden center. Place the cuttings at an angle in the trenches you have made for them, so that they are almost lying on the planting medium, slanting up where the tip will emerge. Cover firmly with some of the sand-peat mixture from the trenches, so only about a third of the cutting is in the open. With all the cuttings in this position, the lid can be fitted on firmly. Remove it daily, as before, so the cuttings can get fresh air and you can check on the moisture of the soil.

If you use several cuttings from one kind of plant, one will be expendable. You can uncover that one in about two weeks, and then as often as you wish, to see how the new roots are coming along. If the cutting does not survive this treatment, try another. Coleus is good for this purpose because it is inexpensive and easily obtained. When roots show strongly, the cuttings are ready to be transplanted from propagating box to flowerpot or window box. Use all-purpose soil in the permanent planter, but leave a little of the sand-and-peat mixture around the roots when you transplant.

B. Reproduction from a cutting of part of a root. Some of the plants readily propagated by this method are crab apple, lilac, raspberry, blackberry, trumpet creeper, bouvardia, and oriental poppy. If you live in the city, a trip to the country could include gathering a few sections of roots and bringing them home wrapped in damp earth and newspaper. If you live in the country, look over your home garden and the gardens of your friends and ask for a root cutting of lilac, raspberry, or whatever is available. If you know a friendly nurseryman, perhaps he will be interested in your experiment and provide a root cutting. Plant it as soon as possible after you get it. Plant the cuttings in large flowerpots, water regularly, and try not to be curious and dig them up before they get settled in and take hold.

C. Propagate a potato plant, using an "eye" of a potato. Cut out a section of the potato that contains the eye, with a generous amount of potato around it. Plant it in a pot, keep it watered, and wait for the first sprout to show.

There are other methods of propagating from part of a plant. For example, you can propagate a new plant from a single leaf of plants such as rex begonia, peperomia, and African violet. If you are interested in going further, do some research at your local library. For a description of propagation by a single leaf, you might start with the book by Montague Free mentioned in the Bibliography at the back of this book.

A display of two or three new plants started by some of these methods, together with your record of procedure, would be an interesting exhibit to take to school.

43. EXPERIMENT

This experiment in the growing of roots on a tree branch is for those living in the country.

Needed: Unmilled sphagnum from a garden center, Saran Wrap or thin plastic, a sharp knife, and heavy string.

Directions: Select a branch of a tree, low enough to work with comfortably and to observe without climbing. Cut away the tree bark in a one-inch strip all around the branch. Wrap unmilled sphagnum around the section of branch where you cut away the bark. Cover the sphagnum with Saran Wrap or plastic. Fasten this covering with cord or string, firmly so it will not slip but not so tightly that it cuts into nearby bark. To make it fit well, you will want the covering to extend a short distance beyond the sphagnum on both sides.

In six weeks, remove the covering. Note and record in detail what has happened to the branch.

44. EXPERIMENT

This project investigates root hairs further than was done in Experiments 33 and 39.

Needed: Radish seeds, a clay flowerpot, and a larger pot or a box. Radish seeds are selected for this experiment because they are easy to obtain and illustrate root hairs well, whereas some plants have few or none.

Directions: Germinate the radish seeds by placing them on the dampened rim of the smaller clay pot. Invert the larger pot or the box over them and dampen them daily with care so they will not become dislodged. Also germinate more radish seeds in a dish, keeping them moist but not swimming in water.

As the seeds progress in germination, note the development of root hairs and compare those on the pot rim and in the dish. Root hairs provide the starting plant with water and nourishment from the soil, for a few days, and then are replaced by regular roots. In your two containers, the root hairs cannot get nourishment from soil, but they will develop to reach water. The root hairs of radish seeds may increase the absorbing surface of a plant as much as twenty times. Observe the root hair system, with hand lens, microscope, or without them. Note in your report that root hairs take over in providing nourishment as the cotyledons dwindle. The root hairs also hold the plant in position until the regular roots form.

45. ACTIVITY

Growing your own citrus plants will not provide new information but will produce attractive plants for gifts or school exhibits.

Needed: Save grapefruit, lemon, and orange seeds as the fruits appear at meals. Get several small plastic pots at the garden center or other store, not smaller than two and a half inches across at the rim. Some pebbles or pieces of clay flowerpots, and pieces of cardboard.

Directions: Put a few pebbles or some pieces of broken clay flowerpot in the bottom of each plastic pot, and then add soil to about three-quarters of an inch from the top. Plant three seeds in each pot, marking the pots to show they contain lemon seeds, tangerine seeds, and so on. Set the pots in a large pan and water them. Cover each pot with a small piece of cardboard. Remove the cardboard each day to make sure the soil is damp. In each pot, use one seed from which you have scratched the coat to let in moisture more quickly. Watch to see whether one seed usually develops faster than the other two in each pot.

When the first sign of action appears above the soil—the tip of a shoot or the curve of a stem which will push up and straighten—remove the cardboard from that pot. Keep the pots in a shady place. For the first few days after uncovering, gradually move the pan of pots into stronger light. As leaves appear, move the pan into sunlight.

Have a few extra pots ready if you want to use the plants for gifts. Otherwise, have a planter ready with soil in place. When the seedlings are strong, about an inch and a half high with well-developed leaves, transplant them, leaving one seedling in each pot. Take plenty of soil with the seedlings and try not to disturb the roots. Settle the remaining seedlings in the center of the pots. They can be more easily moved about if the soil is damp and stays in a ball around the roots.

As the weeks go by, you will have attractive seedlings with glossy leaves in the small pots and perhaps a plantation of them in a planter. You can introduce them to friends by saying, "One day I was eating an orange—" or, "One day I wanted some lemonade—"

46. EXPERIMENT

In this experiment, the rate of transpiration of a plant is measured. Transpiration is the giving off of moisture.

Needed: A tall bottle with a fairly large opening and a cork that fits the opening. A geranium cutting with several leaves attached. Masking tape and a twist drill with a bit large enough to make a one-fourth-inch hole. This hand drill is often called an eggbeater by those unfamiliar with it because it operates in a similar fashion.

Directions: With the twist drill and bit, make a hole in the cork, end to end, that will fit the stem of the cutting. The fit should be fairly close so that there will be little evaporation from the bottle, but not tight enough to pinch the stem or bruise it when it passes through the hole. Paste a strip of masking tape on the bottle, top to bottom, and mark the tape with a line at every one-eighth inch—you will find it simpler to do this before attaching it. Make sure the tape is the right length. Strip off the leaves from the geranium cutting, but leave on half a dozen at the top. Fit the cork over the stem, pushing it up toward the leaves, and almost fill the bottle with water to the top. Now you will see why the wide mouth of the bottle is important, because you will have to put the lower part of the stem in the bottle, well underwater, and cut off a small piece of stem with long scissors. This work with the scissors must be done underwater to prevent air bubbles from forming in the stem. Then immediately slip the cork down till it fits firmly in the neck of the bottle, with about half of the stem underwater. Mark the water level on the tape strip and also note it in your record. Continue to keep a daily record of the water level for at least a week.

You will notice that the water level sinks steadily, although you have closed the bottle with the cork. At the end of a week you will have the total amount of water transpired and also the daily rate.

For a further experiment that you can do in the same way, start the test with two bottles, using a plant with three leaves and one with six leaves. The leaves of the two plants should be roughly the same size. Keep a record of how much faster is the rate of transpiration for the bottle containing the plant with more leaves.

47. EXPERIMENT

You know from Experiment 34 that green plants use their chlorophyll in combination with light to form food material, a process called photosynthesis. How do leaves that are not green, such as Japanese maple, copper beech, red begonia, and red coleus make their food?

Needed: Several red leaves from each of the plants mentioned above. A white saucer with a deep rim and acetone.

Directions: Tear the leaves into small pieces and drop them into the acetone. Do not do this near open flames or heat, as acetone is very inflammable. Allow the leaf fragments to remain immersed for some minutes. Then use an eggbeater to speed up the extraction of the green pigmentation. Beat briskly for three to four minutes. Carefully strain the extract through an old handkerchief.

The acetone-pigment will be colored green by the chlorophyll from the leaf fragments. The green color was masked by the other pigmentation, anthocyanin.

If you allow the red leaf pieces to remain immersed for a few minutes longer in the acetone, you may see some of the red pigmentation gradually seeping out of the leaf fragments. Before pouring the acetone through the handkerchief strainer, let the extract stand for ten minutes. See if you can observe two "tide lines" on the white side of the dish. One will be red, the other greenish.

Save the chlorophyll extract for the next experiment.

48. EXPERIMENT

An important discovery about chlorophyll was made by Sir George Gabriel Stokes in 1864 while he was looking for something else. Stokes was fascinated by the curious ability of some materials to absorb light energy from the light falling upon them. Later these materials reemitted this light energy but at a lower energy level, thus giving off a different color. The color given off depends upon the chemical nature of the material that absorbs the light energy. Stokes called this fluorescence.

You can easily see this effect in the acetone-chlorophyll extract.

Needed: The acetone-chlorophyll extract from the last experiment, a fairly dark room, your father's slide projector, and a clear glass.

Directions: Pour the chlorophyll extract into the glass. Hold the glass in the direct light of the slide projector and notice the color in direct light. Then hold the glass so that you are viewing it and its contents by reflected light against a dark background. What is the color now? You may have to try this a few times before you get good results. Many simple experiments are unsuccessful because of lack of experience in the simple techniques needed.

Sir George Gabriel Stokes wanted a very pure chlorophyll extract for his experiments with fluorescence. In his efforts to purify chlorophyll he discovered that there was more than one chlorophyll. Stokes called these chlorophyll a and chlorophyll b. The chlorophyll in plants is about one-fourth chlorophyll b.

The importance of cotyledons to a plant is brief but vital. We have watched cotyledons, the storehouses of food, lift above the soil to serve as the first leaves of a plant. We know that in some plants cotyledons supply food in the same manner but stay underground. Further facts about cotyledons are brought out in the following experiments.

49. EXPERIMENT

In this experiment you will check the length of time that cotyledons are important to plants.

Needed: Bean seeds (try several different kinds), iodine, and a planter or some form of container.

Directions: Plant at least a dozen bean seeds, three or four of each kind, in your container. Follow the planting procedures of previous projects. If you soak the beans overnight before planting you will speed up germination. On the third day after planting, dig up one bean seed and cut it in half. Test its stored food with a solution of one-half iodine and one-half water. Watch for a showing of blue in part of the half seed. Repeat this test on following days, always noting the increasing amount of color. Continue testing till the seedlings show an inch above the soil. When does the color decrease in the seed? When do the cotyledons appear above the ground? How long do the cotyledons, below and above ground, supply starch to the new plant? Note the results of the iodine tests showing this.

For further information on the time during which the cotyledons are important to the plant, use kidney beans in another test. Plant enough so you can take up a series of them. When a seed shows that germination has started, which means it can be considered also to have started in the other seeds planted at the same time, dig up three seeds and carefully remove the cotyledons. You will recognize them as the fleshy leaflike parts filled with stored plant food. Replant the three seeds from which the cotyledons have been removed.

At least two of them will probably not survive. On the fifth day, take three more seeds, remove the cotyledons, and replant the seeds. All of these seeds should develop into plants, since by this time the growing plant is able to make its own food.

50. EXPERIMENT

Here you will test the importance of cotyledons.

Needed: Eighteen bean seeds and three planters or containers filled with soil. A pad of paper of mixed colors and a sheet of graph paper.

Directions: Plant six beans in each container. After growth has started and the plants show well above the soil, cut one cotyledon off each plant in the first pot and label that pot. Cut both cotyledons off the plants in the second pot and label that pot. Do not cut the cotyledons in the third pot. This will be the control. Measure the height of the tallest plant in each pot, each day. Graph the results, using a base line and strips of colored paper and noting your color code—blue for one pot, pink for another, yellow for the third. Let one inch stand for one day, across the graph. If you have not done a graph before, follow the plan shown in the illustration. In the drawing, the dotted outline stands for a blue slip of paper, the streaked outline for pink, and the plain for yellow.

After keeping the record for some days and filling the graph paper across its widest spread, draw a line across the tops of the tallest slips of colored paper. Which grew best, the plants with two cotyledons, one, or none?

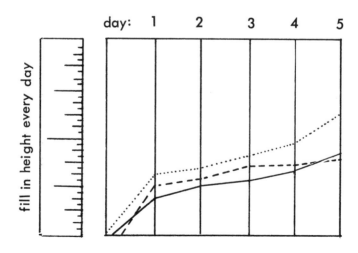

51. EXPERIMENT

Stems of young seedlings are often green, and they carry on photosynthesis as do leaves with chlorophyll. They help provide food in addition to the food from the cotyledons, until the leaves are advanced enough to take over this work. In this experiment, cotyledons, embryos, and stem growth are observed.

Needed: A dozen large seeds such as beans, and India ink.

Directions: Soak the seeds for four to five hours in water. Cut open and examine a seed. A hand lens is helpful but not necessary. The embryo within the seed has a very short stem and is hard to distinguish, but it can be found if the seed is taken apart carefully. You can use tweezers or a toothpick in each hand. The cotyledons are easier to recognize. Note how they are connected to the embryo. In your report of this experiment, sketches will make an interesting sequence. Plant the other seeds and take them up at intervals of two days. Note in the record the growth of the stem and any changes in the appearance of the cotyledons. After the stem of a strong seedling has emerged well above ground and the leaves have started to spread, mark the stem with India ink at regularly spaced intervals. One way to do this is to put the India ink on the stem with the point of a sharpened pencil or a toothpick. Carefully draw the tip across the place on the stem you wish marked.

Note the space between markings, in fractions of an inch, for your record. Now, as the stem grows, observe which section of the stem grows fastest, as will be indicated by the length it stretches between the ink marks. Do you have to keep adding new marks at the top? Where does most of the lengthening of the stem take place?

52. EXPERIMENT

We know from previous experiments that light is important to plants and that they use it for photosynthesis. Light is also important for healthy growth, as is shown in this experiment. Also, you will see how much of the pigmentation of chlorophyll can be developed by the plant without light.

Needed: A dozen seeds of your choice and two seedling trays or containers ready for planting, as described in earlier experiments.

Directions: Plant seeds in both containers. Place one container in a dark closet or carton which lets in no light. Keep the other container in the open to have regular daylight exposure. Water the containers regularly for a week to ten days. By this time, depending on the type of seeds planted, seedlings should be about an inch tall. Now compare the appearance of the seedlings in the two containers.

Note in your report as many points of contrast as possible, such as strength of stem and erectness of seedlings. Note especially the color of the seedlings which grew in darkness. Since you have used the same soil and watered the containers equally, and since the food reserve of the seeds has lasted throughout this period, the differences between the seedlings in the two containers can only come from the presence of light or lack of it during growth. You can make a firm conclusion in your report as to the importance of light to the healthy growth of seedlings. Prove this with points such as the color and ungainly growth of the seedlings grown in darkness.

Continue to keep one plant in darkness for an additional week, never exposing it to light. When the stored plant food is used up, does the plant survive?

The seedlings that grew in the dark will have a bleached look. They are yellowish rather than green. These plants are usually leggy and their stems are tender looking and full of water. If you place these plants in sunlight for a few minutes, then remove them and place them in indirect light, you can find out the number of days it will take for the plants to lose their yellowish cast and gain a healthy greenish appearance.

Differences in plant growth are not entirely due to the presence or absence of chlorophyll. There is a substance in plants that can use light energy to change, chemically, into chlorophyll. Once this change has taken place, the chlorophyll, together with other pigments, can, in the presence of light, start the process of photosynthesis—the making of plant nutrients.

The plant does not need sunlight to manufacture all its pigments. Plant seedlings can manufacture the yellow pigment xanthophyll in darkness, but light is necessary to make the greenish-blue or the yellow-green chlorophyll pigments.

Another pigment present during photosynthesis is one of the carotenoid group. This pigment group got its name from the common carrot's orange color caused by the presence of carotene—one of the carotenoid pigments.

53.   EXPERIMENT

This experiment shows the effect of filtered light on photosynthesis.

Needed: Three plants of the same kind, and large sheets of red, blue, and clear cellophane.

Directions: Cover each plant with two sheets of the same color of cellophane. You will have one plant covered with blue, one with red, and one with clear cellophane. Fasten the cellophane loosely around each pot so the plants appear to be in bags. Cut air holes at top and bottom; keep these small so direct light will not get in.

After three days, remove two leaves from each plant and test them for starch, as in Experiment 25. Compare the results and note in your report the effect of the colors.

54.   EXPERIMENT

The depth at which a seed is planted will affect its germination. In this experiment you will test the effect of depth.

Needed: An old aquarium or a large jar such as a gallon jar with a wide mouth. Two kinds of seeds.

Directions: Plant the mixed seeds inside the glass container near the sides. Start with a two-inch layer of soil over drainage pebbles and place the first seeds. Cover with half an inch of soil. Again scatter seeds near the sides of the container and again cover with soil. Continue till you have four layers of seeds, the top ones lightly covered, the others planted more deeply. Water daily and observe the seed germination through the glass.

What is shown about the depth at which seeds of the same type are planted? Which seeds germinate first? Which do not germinate at all? Using a ruler, measure the depth of the glass from the top down, so you can comment accurately on the depth of different layers of seeds. If you are using a jar instead of an aquarium, make a cradle of wood for it or set it between several bricks so it will not roll out of position.

You have probably heard of grafting plants. This results in two different plants that are joined together, and it can give an interesting effect of contrasting foliage on one plant.

The following two experiments will show you more about grafting. The first uses coleus, a plant with strongly marked leaves. The second grafts two very differently shaped cactus plants to give a dramatic effect.

55. EXPERIMENT

Grafting coleus

Needed: Two coleus plants of different colors, one all green and white, the other with red showing strongly. You will also need a sharp knife, masking tape, and vaseline.

Directions: Cut the center stems of both plants so that in a pattern they will fit each other. (Illustration on page 72.) Work rapidly after cutting because the loss of moisture can mean failure of the graft. Fit the stems together and put a little vaseline around the joining. Tape the two together, starting well below the joining and continuing well above. Tape firmly, but not so tightly that the edges of the tape cut into the stem. If you have used too much vaseline and the tape slips, wipe some off. After the taping is done, spread vaseline over the entire taped area to make sure moisture will not escape.

After several weeks, when you are sure the top part of the plant is growing well, carefully remove the tape by holding the stem firmly in one hand and slicing the tape with a pair of thin-bladed scissors. Or if you left folded tape handles at the end of the binding, you might be able to unwind the tape without any pulling about of the joined stems. If removing the tape proves difficult, leave it in place rather than damage the joining.

Now you have a plant which is one-half leaves of one color, one-half leaves of another color. This gives an unusual effect.

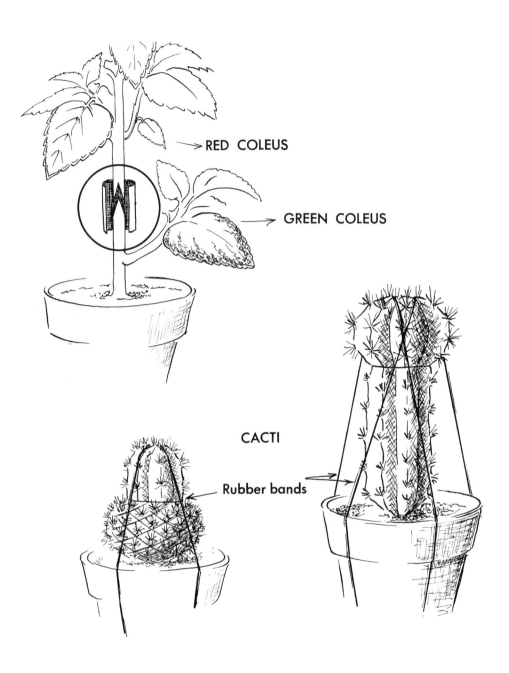

RED COLEUS

GREEN COLEUS

CACTI

Rubber bands

56.   EXPERIMENT

Grafting cacti

Needed: Two cactus plants of contrasting appearance, with a thick rather than slender shape. A sharp knife; a small pointed clipper type of tool, which can be professional snippers or manicure clippers; rubber bands of various sizes; a pair of tweezers; a long needle; and a hand lens.

Directions: The simplest way to graft cacti is to follow the flat method. First, cut each plant through at the point you select for the graft; for example, the base plant or stock, which will always be larger, might have the top quarter removed, and the plant which will form the new top, called the scion, would have a quarter or less of its top removed for joining, depending on the size of this plant. Next, use the knife to trim the two sections near the cut areas, leveling any rough spots and smoothing rib corners where the joining will be made. With clippers or knife, remove any spines overhanging the cut areas that would interfere with the joining. By this time you might want to use the needle and tweezers to remove any spines that may have caught your fingers. Now fit the two sections together—the large bottom section and the smaller tip of the other plant. Make sure there is a close fit, trimming as necessary. Also make sure that the new top is level, the center of its growth in a top-middle position so it will grow straight.

The final step should be done quickly. Sterilize the knife in boiling water and cut very thin slices from the end of each cut section you are using. The slices must be so thin there is no new roughness or unevenness. You must slice rather than saw. The two sections should now fit as well as before. If not, trim to fit and try again after cutting off two very thin slices. Place the sections together and fasten them in position with rubber bands, as shown in the illustration. The two sections should be held together firmly, but the rubber bands should not be too tight. In working with the sections, small ice tongs may be used with care and heavy leather gloves may be tried. But the simplest way is to work doggedly with your uncovered fingers, removing the spines from them

73

when necessary. The unusual plant resulting from the graft should be worth a few annoying spines in the hands.

Check the elastic bands to see that they are holding the sections together evenly without too much pressure at any point. For the first try at grafting, it is helpful to choose a cactus for the stock that has some large downward-pointing spines to which you can hook the rubber bands that are looped over the scion. With other cacti, the rubber bands can be hooked around the bottom of the pot. Water very sparingly and do not let water touch the graft's union point. If rot shows at the union in a few days, separate the two plants and slice and join again, as before. A successful graft should unite in about a week. If the graft is made outdoors in warm weather, the rubber bands will eventually rot away. If they do not, they can be cut off after the graft unites. An outdoor graft should be covered by a large paper bag for a few days.

When you have made a successful graft, you will have a dramatic plant with strikingly different sections.

This next experiment is for microscope users only.

57. EXPERIMENT

The purpose of this experiment is to examine the stomata which you observed in Experiment 40. You will also be able to see the irregularly shaped epidermal cells of the skin layer.

Needed: A plant leaf—a begonia leaf is particularly easy to work with; a microscope slide; and a cover slip, if possible.

Directions: Cut off a very thin cross section of the leaf and place it in a drop of water on the slide. If you have a cover slip, use it now. Look through the microscope and then draw the stomata, or mouthlike openings, in the leaf. These openings are formed by pairs of cells that look kidney-shaped. Sketch some of the epidermal cells.

Now try the same test with leaves of other plants. If possible, cut a thin slice of leaf and arrange it on a slide so a cross section is in view. If you find any interesting differences between the leaves of the two kinds of plants, describe them and name the plants.

Long-term Experiments and Activities

Long-term projects need patience and often a careful precision in following through a given experiment, but they are rewarding. They can be combined well with shorter projects. You can be making an additional hotbed, or starting a good supply of seedlings, or doing several short experiments while a long project runs its course.

It is especially helpful to start seedlings at an early date. Seeds can be planted in small containers for a hotbed, or in a series of paper cups that will rest in a hotbed, or in a shallow box lined with aluminum foil. Remember to make some drainage holes in each cup.

Select a variety of seeds and mark the cups or containers so you will know later which seedlings are which. Marigold seedlings emerge above the soil in about five days and are sturdy. Select some other kinds of flower seeds and do your own experimenting, keeping a record of the time needed for germination and for the seedlings to get tall enough for use in experiments. Be sure to plant some beans and peas also. If you use scarlet runner beans, you will have vines with red flowers after you have finished experimenting with seedlings.

Some of the experiments will need very young seedlings and others, larger ones. You will be ready at any time if you plant seeds in two paper cups, wait a week and plant seeds in two more cups, and continue planting seeds at intervals so there will be an array of seedlings of different sizes. Be sure to make some drainage holes in each cup.

You might also start a supply of new plants from cuttings, as described in Experiment 42. Later, when an experiment calls for a coleus plant, for example, you will have several to choose from.

Seedlings and cuttings progress fairly rapidly. So you can watch them coming along while you do some of the following long-term experiments.

58. EXPERIMENT

The strength of growing roots is shown in this experiment. It was worked out by a student.

Needed: Seeds, such as sweet William seed, and half an eggshell.

Directions: Fill half an eggshell with soil, leaving a little space at the top for easy watering. Sprinkle seeds across the top, covering with soil. Follow directions on the package, as the depth of planting may vary with the type of seed. Spray regularly with water, using the plunger type of spray mentioned earlier or one of the other devices suggested. Don't water so heavily that the soil gets soggy. Balance the eggshell firmly, by any method you prefer, such as fitting it into a hollow in the earth at the top of a flowerpot. Place in sunlight. As the seedlings develop, you can use a little more water. In four or five weeks, the eggshell will begin to crack. Gradually, through the following days, it will fall apart. Inspect the remains of the shell and you will see that the seedling roots, now large and strong, have demolished the eggshell.

Keep the other half of the eggshell filled with earth and in another hollow near the first eggshell, possibly in the same flowerpot. Water it also even though it has no seeds that you know of. Should some plant start growing, pluck it out immediately for this second eggshell is to be your control. After the first eggshell has been cracked apart by the strength of the growing root systems of the young seedlings, you can also carefully check the second unplanted eggshell. Has its shell also been split? What, then, is responsible for the breaking apart of the first eggshell? Mention in your report other instances of roots thrusting, twisting, and pushing, such as the cracking of sidewalk slabs of concrete.

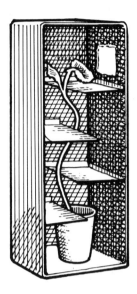

59.   EXPERIMENT

Making and operating a plant maze is a classic experiment that maintains its interest.

Needed: A shoe box with a cover, cardboard, glue, and a small climbing plant.

Directions: Cut three pieces of cardboard, each about two-thirds the width of the shoe box plus an extra inch. Bend each piece an inch from one end, across a ruler or a table edge, to make a neat angle. Glue these one-inch tabs to the sides of the shoe box, so the cardboard pieces reach out straight like shelves. There will be two on one side, top and bottom, with the third piece in the middle between the other two, as illustrated. You will see in the drawing that the shelves slightly overlap an imaginary center line and that the ends where the tabs are glued on extend all across the sides where they are attached. With the box set on end, mark a spot two inches above the top shelf on the side where it is attached. At this point, cut out a round hole about an inch in diameter to provide light for the plant. The shelves—called baffles—will prevent the direct growth of the plant toward the light. On the bottom of the box at the side away from the open front, glue a strip of cardboard so the box will rest level when the lid is on.

Now place the plant in its pot on the bottom of the box, in the open space beyond the first baffle so that it will start to grow up around the baffle. Put on the cover, making sure it is a tight fit. Close it with tape if necessary so the only light in the box comes from the high window you have cut. Light will filter down to the plant around the baffles. Unlike the box in Experiment 5, which had several windows, this box has only one, and you can expect this experiment to take longer. But as you remove the lid to water the plant daily, you will see how determinedly it is working around the baffles to find its way up toward the single source of light.

After several weeks, you will see the tip of the plant starting out of the window. When it is well outside, you can leave the lid off to show the whole pattern of growth.

60. EXPERIMENT

In this experiment, cuttings are grown to show a variety of foliage, all started in water.

Needed: Two beets, two carrots, two turnips, your choice of English ivy, joint plant, and coleus; dishes with high rims; a planter or other container; and a glass jar.

Directions: Trim off the old leaves from the beets, carrots, and turnips, leaving an inch of stem. Cut the roots so each forms a two-inch strip attached to the short stem. Now you have the short tops of carrots, for example, with handles of stems. Set these tops in dishes, with either shallow water or pebbles under them so the water does not cover them. Place the cuttings of ivy, coleus, and joint plant in a jar of water. New foliage will grow from the vegetable sections. The cuttings will produce roots and start to grow.

The vegetable sections will grow short roots but not new taproots. When foliage is well advanced and roots well formed, place all the sections and cuttings in the planter. You will have a foliage display, showing what can be done with a portion of a plant and water.

61. EXPERIMENT

Here you will compare the growth of seeds in a variety of nutrients.

Needed: Ten lima bean seeds, five dishes with high rims, salt, sugar, honey, and cornstarch.

Directions: Dissolve sugar in water in one dish, salt in another, cornstarch in another, and mix honey and water in the fourth. The fifth dish will contain only water and is the control. Label each dish according to its contents. Soak the beans overnight. Carefully take out the embryo of each seed. Put two embryos in each dish. Keep the dishes in the light but not in direct sunlight.

Keep a record of how the embryos in each dish progress, noting the differences among them.

62. EXPERIMENT

This experiment is best done in the country, but city dwellers can collect soil on a country trip. A comparison will be made between the fertility of topsoil and subsoil.

Needed: Two flowerpots full of topsoil from two locations and two of subsoil, also from different locations. A trowel for digging the soil. The subsoil should be taken from a depth of at least a foot and a half. Bean seeds or other seeds you have used before; familiarity with their stages of development will help you.

Directions: Plant the seeds in the pots, which should be labeled as to type of soil and its source, such as meadow or woods. Give the pots the same amount of water and sunshine.

As the seeds develop, keep records showing the comparative speed of growth, health, strength, and any other details you observe. After the experiment is over, take two small envelopes of soil from each of the four pots. Label each envelope carefully as to type of soil and where it came from: for example, subsoil meadow or topsoil woods. Send one set of the four envelopes to the nearest agricultural station and request a soil analysis. Explain why you wish the results and tell about your experiment. Use the other four samples yourself. Purchase a soil testing kit, follow the instructions, compare your results with those of the professionals.

63. EXPERIMENT

The stages in the growth of a seedling are shown clearly in an exhibit that might be called a demonstration in five acts.

Needed: Five large seeds. The avocado is a good choice because its seeds have a large quantity of stored food that will last well in the test. So you might ask for avocado salad at dinner and save the seeds. You will also need five jars or large glasses and some toothpicks.

Directions: You are going to start these avocado seeds growing one after the other, with intervals between starting so each will always be in a different stage of growth. Start the first seed by taking off the papery brown coat and placing it in the neck of a jar of water, pointed end up. It should rest in the top of the jar, with only the bottom part in the water. If the neck of the jar is too wide, support the seed with toothpicks inserted in the seed with the free end of the toothpicks resting on the rim of the jar. Keep the seed in a dim light while the roots start growing and keep enough water in the jar to cover a third of the seed. When the roots

Growing avocado seeds in jars.

have started and the stem starts to grow, move the jar into stronger light. Move it gradually into sunlight. Note the length of time between starting the seed and moving it into stronger light. This will be the fixed time period between the starting of each seed.

Start the remaining seeds in the same way, one by one, with the time interval you have noted between each. By the time you have the last one started, the first will be flourishing with a strong stem, green leaves, and a mass of roots.

Place the jars in a row, from the smallest to the largest. As they grow, you will have an exhibit showing growth at different stages.

Experiments from Darwin

Many of the experiments you have seen here and many of those you will do at school and read about in books listed in the Bibliography originated long ago. A surprising number of them can be traced back directly to Charles Darwin. Some of these you will find in a book by Darwin, *The Movements and Habits of Climbing Plants,* published in 1870 in England.

Before Darwin did his intensive research on plants, it was generally held that a major difference between plants and animals was that plants had no power of movement. Darwin changed this belief.

He wrote, "It has often been vaguely asserted that plants are distinguished from animals by not having the power of movement. It should rather be said that plants acquire and display this power only when it is of some advantage to them." But whether or not plants behave as do animals to outside stimuli is open to discussion.

One of Darwin's friends, plant scientist Dr. Asa Gray, said this of Darwin's work: "He was a scientific investigator—a philosopher, if you please, but one of the type of Galileo. Indeed very much what Galileo was to physical science in his time, Darwin is to biological science in ours." Charles Darwin was the first to set forth the basic idea of the present hormone theory of tropisms. One biographer later commented that for over thirty-three years after Darwin's death no new progress had been made beyond the areas he investigated. The following experiments are based on Darwin's work and follow his directions and conclusions.

64. EXPERIMENT

Darwin observed that twining plants had an independent movement —revolving in a circle. This is more easily seen at the tip of the plants, but the entire climbing shoot can also be seen to move in a circle. This experiment will show the revolving action of a twining plant.

Needed: For this experiment and the next one, select twining plants from this list: kidney bean, pea, wisteria, hop, honeysuckle, and morning glory. You will also need some stamp-pad ink and a small paint brush.

Directions: Choose a twining plant of good size. Paint a streak along one side from top to bottom with the stamp-pad ink and brush. One side of the plant will be convex or bowed out, and the streak should go along this side. Examine the plant every day for a few days.

The colored streak will be seen to become twisted around the stem like the red line on a barber's pole. It will run on the convex and concave sides of the stem. The revolving movement has been described as a continuous bowing to all points of the compass.

65. EXPERIMENT

This experiment demonstrates the revolving action of the tip of a twining plant—a movement that is clearly observable.

Needed: A plant of good size from the above list. Also, a broom straw, a plastic soda straw, glue, and a slide projector.

Directions: Glue the broom straw to a short piece of the soda straw. Carefully slip this sleeve of plastic straw, with broom straw attached, over the tip of the growing shoot. Borrow a slide projector or take the plant to someone who has a slide projector. Place the plant on a table so that its shadow, showing shoot with the attached straws, falls clearly on a wall. Watch the tip movement for an hour or so.

You can make a graph of this movement for your record if you fasten a piece of paper to a large cardboard box and place this box on the wall end of the table where it will catch the shadow. Mark the paper with a dot at regular intervals of time, to show the changing position of tip and straws. The series of dots will give you a graph of the tip movement if you connect the points with a line. Be sure to turn on the slide projector only when you wish to mark or observe the shadows of the straws on the paper or wall.

66. EXPERIMENT

The effect of light on the rotating motion of a twining plant is shown in this experiment.

Needed: A plant of good size from the above list. A strong light.

Directions: Place the plant in a dark room with no other light except from your one strong source. The light should be at one side of the plant. Time the circular rotation of the plant as it approaches the light and as it turns away from it. The plant will make its usual revolving movement in the usual period of time. However, when the tip approaches the light, its movement will speed up. When the tip turns away from the light, its movement will slow down.

You may want to compare this result with the usual rotation of the plant in normal light which surrounds it on all sides. In normal light the plant revolves comparatively evenly.

TO RECORD PLANT ROTATION

shadow of
revolving tip

tilt projector upwards

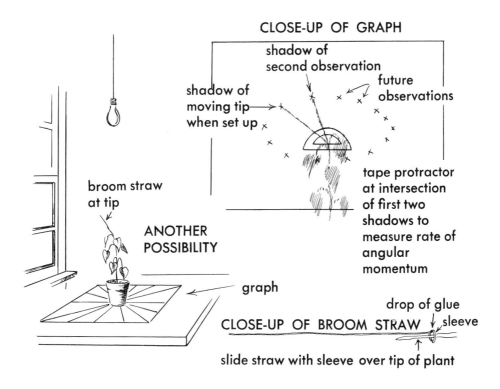

CLOSE-UP OF GRAPH

shadow of
second observation

future
observations

shadow of
moving tip →
when set up

tape protractor
at intersection
of first two
shadows to
measure rate of
angular
momentum

broom straw
at tip

ANOTHER
POSSIBILITY

graph

drop of glue

CLOSE-UP OF BROOM STRAW   sleeve

slide straw with sleeve over tip of plant

67. EXPERIMENT

In this experiment you can test for yourself Darwin's research showing that plant movement can be affected by weather conditions or by merely moving a plant from one location to another, as well as by shaking it for a few seconds. Some scientists are interested in how solar storms—sunspot activity—affect plants. You can experiment with this yourself.

Needed: Select two plants of different kinds from the above list. One of these should be a kidney bean plant.

Directions: Settle the plants in a place from which they will not have to be moved. Watch the weather reports and the barometer. During the time of a thunderstorm and of a falling barometer, observe the plants. These observations may be very difficult unless you again use the slide projector and the wall-shadow technique. On a piece of paper attached to the wall, mark a shadow outline of the main stem positions. Shut off the slide projector's light until the storm or bad weather is well under way and make another drawing, in a different color ink or crayon, after turning on the slide projector once again for a few seconds.

You might also do a test to find out whether a week of excessive sunspot activity affects the period of revolution of the plants being tested. This activity of plants was noticed long after Darwin's work, but it is interesting because it is another external factor affecting plant movement. Here you will need your previous records of the usual period of revolution for the plants being tested so that you can make accurate comparisons. Sunspot activity seems to run in eleven-year cycles. Observatories, planetariums, and the teletype services are usually very aware of peak periods of such activity. Very often such excessive electromagnetic sunspot disturbances are noted in the news bulletins as a matter of routine. These times are the peak activity and you will obtain any really observable results then. These disturbances often last for several weeks or more—ample time for you to make observations. Although much remains to be learned about sunspots, scientists do know that they affect our weather, which in turn affects the organic life of this planet. You may not see any results at all, but try it for fun.

68. EXPERIMENT

This experiment follows Darwin's work on traumatropism, which is the turning away of a plant from a source of injury. Darwin discovered that roots possessed the ability to turn aside from an object that was doing harm to them.

Needed: Large seeds such as kidney or lima beans. Two needles, pins and corks, and a wire of medium thickness.

Directions: Germinate several seeds, following the pin-in-a-cork method shown in the illustration. Watch for root development. When a root starts downward, place a needle point in the direct path of the root. Fasten the needle so that the growing root will run into its sharp point. With another root, insert a needle point a short way into the root. Do this near the root tip for best results. Watch how the roots withdraw in time from these sharp menaces and then resume their downward path.

Heat a piece of wire until it is red hot at one end. With this hot tip, very lightly touch the roots of several seedlings. Touch the roots very quickly and lightly near the tips and on one side. These roots will eventually turn away from the direction of the lightly burned spot—the source of harm having come from that area.

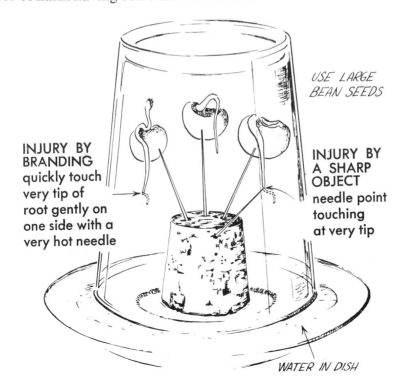

USE LARGE
BEAN SEEDS

INJURY BY
BRANDING
quickly touch
very tip of
root gently on
one side with a
very hot needle

INJURY BY
A SHARP
OBJECT
needle point
touching
at very tip

WATER IN DISH

You as the Scientist

Many of the experiments and activities in the previous section were done at home. You could often add your own personal variations to the projects. Sometimes you worked out a new experiment to check a result.

Activities can usually be given an individual flavor. A hotbed can have a special shade to be pulled down across its window. You might try stringing beans besides navy marrow beans. The terrarium can be built especially high, with room for carnivorous plants that stretch tall.

Here are some additional comments about the experiments and activities discussed. Carnivorous plants are sufficiently varied for you to plan unusual effects with them in your terrarium. The cobra lily, for instance, is a tall plant with a head like the cobra snake. Parrot pitchers have heads like the cobra lilies but without the appearance of fangs; they are shorter plants, up to six inches in height. Huntsman's-horn has an interesting lid over its top, and this plant, like the cobra lily, can reach a height of twenty-four inches. Northern pitcher plants are green when they are small and turn red as they grow. These do not get much higher than six inches. Still smaller plants are the sundew, butterwort, and Venus's-flytrap. All of these will catch insects.

If you would like to try a modern experiment, order some carnivorous plants that have been irradiated with gamma rays from cobalt 60. You can get these from the supplier listed in the back of the book. Also listed in that suppliers' catalog are other plants subjected to atomic radiation, such as garden vegetables which grew unusually large or fat or tall and which, in addition, very often have unusual coloration. Some of these plants will produce offspring that may be mutants—plants unusually different in size, shape, or color. You cannot be sure that something unusual is a mutation, but the chance is increased several thousand times by irradiation.

Part of scientific work is following in another scientist's footsteps, learning the routes, the reasons, and the results. And part is going out yourself on a path you hope will be new.

You might find a mutation, or change in a plant that makes it different from any other plant of its type. This would be your own discovery. Other new paths could lead to the creation of a new plant or flower by the technique of hybridization. This needs care and patience but is not too difficult. John James' book on the creation of new flowers and plants is listed in the Bibliography. If you will get it from the library, you can find out how to do it for yourself.

There is trial and error in the new method. An experiment may not work the first time, nor the sixth time. But by analyzing what was wrong, learning from mistakes, realizing the value of careful techniques, and then trying again, success becomes a personal achievement.

Scientists in their laboratories expect to try again. They study their records, learn everything they can, and keep on trying. As in any exploration, there is the challenge of the journey and the pride in arrival.

Student scientists can find the same challenge and the same pride. The key word is *why*. Why do growing things show certain ways and methods and variations? On the road to finding out is *how*. As in a detective story, if you work on the *how*, sooner or later you will reach the *why*.

There is a great deal of question asking in science. The more curiosity you have about the working of things and the reason for things, the better.

As you try an experiment or an activity, you will see the pattern to follow, and soon you will be racing through the written directions, knowing quickly how to set up a project. As you continue your work, you will find a familiar method, just as you mark out a path by frequent walking.

Part of this method is a habit of care. If you plant a seed too deep, this will probably be the end of it. Another part is the willingness to repeat an experiment if the first try does not turn out right. Yet another part is keeping an accurate record. If you succeed in growing a new kind of plant but have no record of how you did it, your success loses part of its value. Records written up later always lose their sharpness of vision and sensitivity. Be accurate first, and neat when you have the time. And for the student scientist working at home, an important part is explaining to the family that their helpful interest is appreciated but their taking over any of the thinking out of a problem would hurt the scientist's own achievement.

When you do a project yourself, you make it your own. What you find out from an experiment is quite different from being told the result. You want to know, and you find out for yourself. This is an attitude that is part of our modern living.

As Professor Vernet Eaton of Wesleyan University says, "This is an age of science. Ninety percent of all the scientists who ever lived are alive today."

Bibliography

BUDLONG, WARE, *Indoor Gardens*. New York, Hawthorn, 1967.

COOPER, ELIZABETH K., *Insects and Plants — The Amazing Partnership*. New York, Harcourt, Brace and World, 1963.

DICKERSON, ALICE, *The First Book of Plants*. New York, Franklin Watts, 1953.

DODGE, BERTHA S., *Plants That Changed the World*. Boston, Little Brown, 1959.

FENTON, CARROLL L., AND KITCHEN, HERMINE B., *Plants That Feed Us*. New York, John Day, 1956.

HAMMOND, WINIFRED G., *The Riddle of Seeds*. New York, Coward-McCann, 1966.

HUTCHINS, ROSS E., *Amazing Seeds*. New York, Dodd, Mead, 1965.

————, *Plants Without Leaves*. New York, Dodd, Mead, 1966.

————, *This Is a Leaf*. New York, Dodd, Mead, 1962.

HYDE, MARGARET O., *Plants Today and Tomorrow*. New York, McGraw-Hill, 1960.

JAMES, JOHN, *Create New Flowers and Plants*. New York, Doubleday, 1964.

KLEIN, DRS. RICHARD AND DEANA, *Discovering Plants*. Garden City, N.Y., Natural History Press, 1968.

LANE, FERDINAND C., *All About the Flowering World*. New York, Random House, 1956.

LLOYD, F. E., *Carnivorous Plants*. New York, Ronald Press, 1942.

POOLE, LYNN AND GRAY, *Insect Eating Plants*. New York, Crowell, 1963.

RASKIN, EDITH, *Fantastic Cactus, Indoors and Out*. New York, Lothrop, 1968.

SELSAM, MILLICENT, *Plants That Heal*. New York, William Morrow, 1959.

————, *Plants We Eat*. New York, William Morrow, 1955.

————, *Play with Plants*. New York, William Morrow, 1949.

STEFFERUD, ALFRED, *Wonders of Seeds*. New York, Harcourt, Brace and World, 1956.

ZIM, HERBERT S., *What's Inside of Plants*. New York, William Morrow, 1952.

Appendix

Sources of Supplies

Geo. W. Park Seed Co., Greenwood, South Carolina 29646: Basic garden supplies plus kits for "Instant Beauty." Control chemicals for growth experiments.

Arthur Eames Allgrove, North Wilmington, Massachusetts 01887: Terrarium supplies, insectivorous plants, booklets, books and bulletins. Request 25¢ bulletin, "The Register," which lists plants as well as terrarium kits, etc.

Cornell Science Packets, Building 7, Cornell University Research Park, Ithaca, New York 14850: Request bulletin which lists publications, many of which are free. Pamphlets can be purchased individually for 25¢ or in packets for approximately $2.25 per packet. Packet A ($2) is mainly about plants.

Oak Ridge Atom Industries, Education Products Division, 500 Elza Drive, P.O. Box 429, Oak Ridge, Tennessee: Seeds and vegetables, flowers exposed to radiation from cobalt 60. Unusual sizes, colors, etc., are the usual result. Mutants are common. Kits cost $3 and up.

Hankscraft Company, Reedsburg, Wisconsin: Supplies small 6–9 volt battery-driven, rotating display sign motors. A request may result in an individual order if you carefully specify the nature of usage so that the company can fulfill your order.

Mr. Harry E. Saier, Dimondale, Michigan 48821: Request information. A source for compass plants or the seeds of same, as well as other unusual plants.

Edmund Scientific Company, 403 Edscorp Building, Barrington, New Jersey 08007: Source for strong magnets needed for experiments mentioned in book. Request catalog.

Bausch and Lomb, Rochester, New York: Makes a 100 X microscope with plastic casing, a fine enough instrument for the beginner. With some microscopes it is possible to shine a light source into the reflecting mirror at the bottom and use the instrument as a slide projector.

Nature and Science Magazine, Natural History Press, Garden City, New York 11531: A constant source of experiments and activities. Tells explicitly the materials and construction methods needed to consummate the experiments successfully. Published by the American Museum of Natural History. Many articles are written by scientists actively involved in exciting research areas who pass on to the young readers a sense of discovery about to come.

Index

The Authors

Ware Budlong has had experience both as a teacher and as a writer. Her writing accomplishments include work as a feature writer, foreign correspondent, book review columnist, magazine writer, and book author. Mrs. Budlong's interest in science, particularly in the area of plant life, has been demonstrated by her writings on natural science and by her memberships in horticultural societies.

Mark H. Fleitzer is a specialist in elementary school science in Rye, New York, and holds advanced degrees in education. Mr. Fleitzer is a member of the National Science Teachers Association, as well as of other science and educational groups, and in 1966–67 was the recipient of a National Science Foundation Fellowship. Among his hobbies are fishing, woodworking, golf, art, music, and writing—and science.

JUN. 1 3 1996 DATE DUE			
MAR 09			
MAR 20 20			
JUN 1 1 20			
APR 2 9 2013			